Retiring Tl

Retiring
The Olé Way

The Young Retiree's Guide
to Enjoying Life in Spain

Sue Walker

*To Mum, who seems to have passed on
her "writing genes", and to Steve.*

Thanks for the memories.

Author's Note

First of all I would like to thank Debs Jenkins and Joe Gregory for taking a chance on me and publishing my book in 2009 as part of the Native Spain series of expat titles. They helped to make my long-held dream of being a published author come true, for which I am eternally grateful.

Special thanks to Debs for allowing me to use her original artwork, which I loved as soon as I saw it, for this new edition of my book. I also thank Debs for her helpful suggestions in her role as editor of the first edition.

Next I would like to thank Vicky McGinlay for her expertise as copy editor for this revised edition of my book, and Mark McGinlay for the help he has promised me in promoting it! Any mistakes or inconsistencies are my fault for ignoring Vicky's professional advice. I can't leave Kate McGinlay out, so thanks to Katie for using her catering and cocktail making skills whenever she visits us in our new home in Spain. Obviously she is always welcome here!

Finally, special thanks go to my husband John and our adopted Spanish dog Lisa, both for sharing my new life in Spain and also for allowing me to hog the PC while revising my book!

Contents

PROLOGUE

Where Are We Now?

This is a book without an ending. All I can give you is an unfinished chapter, as it is still very much a work in progress. The intention is to summarise our experiences to date, and to look forward as well as to look back. What are the important lessons that we have learnt? Do we have any pearls of wisdom to impart that will help you, if you plan to embark on a similar journey? (Probably not!) What are our plans, hopes and possible fears for the future?

My husband John and I started with only a vague idea of what we wanted to do and where we wanted to live once we retired. I wouldn't go as far as to say that we were disillusioned with life in the UK, but having lived in south-east England for twenty-eight years and having worked in or near London for over twenty years, I for one wanted to get out of the rat race and start a new life somewhere where the pace of life was slower. John had been planning to work until he was sixty-five, but having had a change of job, and with lots of new courses coming up, he felt that it was time to call it a day. He didn't see the point of money being wasted on courses when he would not be able to get the most out of them. The idea of living in the sun, with time to follow other interests, also appealed to him.

We didn't rush into our decision. We weighed up the pros and cons of the different places that we thought we would like to live in, and eventually ended up with a shortlist of one: Spain.

As Spain is such a vast country, with so many different regions that we had visited already and both knew and loved, it took time to decide exactly where we wanted to live. We researched areas that we hadn't considered before, went on numerous viewing trips over a period of several years and eventually found somewhere where we both felt that we could live quite happily.

We had drawn up a checklist of our requirements, and made sure that the estate agents that showed us round knew exactly what we were looking for. In spite of this, we went on a couple of viewing trips that were, quite frankly, a waste of both our time and theirs. When we eventually found both a property and location that the two of us loved, we thought that was the end of the story. In fact, it was only the beginning.

I am writing this in Jumilla, a small town in the Spanish province of Murcia, which is renowned for its wine. John and I thought that the best aspect of living in Jumilla would be the wine, or perhaps the sunshine, or the relaxed way of life, however we quickly discovered that it is the people. Jumillanos are friendly and welcoming, and although we have only been living here a few months, whenever we walk around the town somebody recognises us and says "Hola", "Buenos días" or even (especially the children) "Hello".

As I begin this chapter John has just retired, so in theory we will now both be living a life of leisure. Fat chance! We have the keys to the apartment that we are renting in Jumilla for nine months, where we are now living. We had expected to be living in our own house by now: read on to find out why our plans have changed.

However we still have a maisonette in London to sell and before it is sold we have a lot of clearing out to do. I have to confess to being a bit of a hoarder, and over the last sixteen years of living with John I have accumulated many treasures (which John rudely refers to as rubbish). I will have to be ruthless and only keep the essentials, but it is going to be a tough task. Books, clothes, CDs and various mementoes will have to be sorted out and I suspect that the resulting heavy bags will give the bin men hernias.

Before we finally leave the UK there will be various financial matters to finalise. Which bank accounts, store cards and credit cards will we retain? Standing orders and debit directs will have to be cancelled, as our gym memberships aren't worth keeping on for the occasional visit to London, and magazine subscriptions also need to be stopped or at least be updated so that they are sent to our new address.

We are planning to complete the move to Spain by the end of 2009, however once that happens we will not be sitting down quietly with a glass of wine and good book, as that is not our style. We both want to work on our own projects, we hope to keep on running and become involved in the Jumilla Athletic Club, and no doubt we will have a constant stream of visitors to entertain.

In fact, we have just said goodbye to our first visitors: John's daughter Sarah, her husband Jerry and their four sons, aged between four and ten. I asked Simon, the eldest, what he liked best about Spain and he said, "Everything, apart from the strawberry jam", which incidentally he had selected when we were out shopping. Joshua made his opinion very clear, "Spain is wicked!" Adam and Elliot also enjoyed themselves, possibly because of the sweets and lollipops handed to them wherever we went. Even the most surly looking waiter or shop assistant seemed to melt when they saw the four blond haired boys. No matter how noisy the children were, they were welcomed everywhere with beaming smiles.

I have to admit that we have had a bit of a roller-coaster ride on our journey, and there have been a few moments of despair as well as many moments of joy. So fasten your seat belts and hold on tightly as you join us on our journey, as it may be a bit of a bumpy ride.

CHAPTER ONE

Where In The World?

Five years ago, John and I started talking about retiring overseas. You know what it's like: the newspapers are full of horror stories illustrating how the country is going downhill; we have a typically British rain-sodden summer; prices are rising all the time; there is a tube strike so the dreadful journey to work gets even worse – it's time to get out of here! I'm sure that strikes a chord with many people, but in our case it wasn't just talk, as we made the decision to buy what seemed to be our dream home in Santa Ana del Monte, just outside the southern Spanish town of Jumilla, which is famous for its wine.

John and I met when we were in our mid to late forties through the central London running club that we belong to. We had both been married before and were divorced by the time we met, and our children are all adults. As well as enjoying running, we love to travel and have similar tastes in music, however I was a vegetarian at the time (I now eat fish) whereas John is a keen carnivore. In spite of that we started living together over sixteen years ago, though as John does most of the cooking, I don't have to worry too much about handling meat. (On the rare occasions when I am doing the cooking, John usually ends up with pasta, though I am considerate enough to let him have meat-filled pasta!)

John had joined the Metropolitan Police as a civilian, having served in the Army for twenty-two years and after taking a couple of years off doing other jobs in between. He enjoyed his job and was lucky enough to work locally so didn't have the hassle of commuting into central London. He was quite happy to continue working until he was sixty-five although as a civil servant he could have retired at sixty.

I like variety and new challenges. After many different jobs over the years, including work as a computer programmer and systems analyst, I changed direction and started a career in Personnel.

Three years ago I decided I wanted to cut down my hours and work part-time, as by then I had qualified as a complementary therapist and I wanted to spend more time on my business. Trying to work full-time, give treatments to clients after work and at weekends, go running a couple of times a week, and also fit in a social life, can be a bit tiring and I was now in my fifties. I thought it was time to take life a bit easier. I eventually found a part-time administrative job at the Royal College of Physicians, which allowed me two or three days a week to work for myself.

I have been a Reflexologist for nearly nine years and qualified as a Bowen therapist just over three years ago. As well as being an Indian Head Massage therapist, I have completed a Seated Acupressure course and numerous workshops ranging from "Reflexology with Hot Stones" to "Thai Foot and Hand Massage". My aim was to retire once I was over sixty and concentrate on being a complementary therapist. As I worked in central London and had to face overcrowded tubes every day, there was no real incentive to continue in an office job, even though I enjoyed working at the College and had great colleagues.

As you have no doubt realised by now, John is the sensible, steady one in our relationship and I am the one who likes to change direction and try out new things. Although we have very different personalities we don't argue much, mainly because John is usually easy-going. I think it is a good combination and certainly stops us getting bored in our relationship.

Choosing A Location

One thing we were both in agreement with was that, once we retired, we would move out of London and look for a new home together in the sun. We wanted a better climate and a more relaxed lifestyle, though we both had plans to keep ourselves busy. I would work part-time as a complementary therapist, which I enjoy so much that it doesn't seem like work, and John would set up running holidays with a difference.

John was Chairman of the largest running club in London, with 2,400 members, so he had a large pool of potential holidaymakers. Certainly when he told people about the running/cycling/walking/sightseeing/wine tasting holidays he planned to organise, there was a lot of interest. Personally, I think it was the wine tasting that was the major selling point!

Initially we weren't sure exactly where we wanted to move. Over the years we had visited many different countries, as John had been in the Army and I had been a Wren, so we had both experienced living and working overseas as well as visiting places on holiday.

At one stage we seriously considered Australia: good climate, they speak the same language, the people are friendly – that can't be bad. However we discovered that, if we retired there, our pensions would not be index linked. We realised that as neither of us would have a huge pension or vast sums of money to invest, it wouldn't be a good choice for us financially - unless of course our lottery numbers came up. Although we both hoped to work, we were not going to rely on that when calculating our finances and planning our move. Too many people move overseas with grand plans that sadly don't come to fruition and they are forced to sell up and return to the UK. We didn't want to become part of that group.

We realised how important it is to spend time deciding which country you want to move to. Living in a country is not the same as going on holiday there, as we both knew from our own experiences. We drew up a checklist of factors that were important to us, some of which I have already mentioned: good climate, friendly people, a relaxed way of life, and somewhere affordable so that we could enjoy a comfortable standard of living. As we both have families, our preference was to be close enough to the UK for them to visit us on a regular basis and for us to make the occasional trip back to see them. This also meant that we needed a reasonably sized property with at least two bedrooms for when family visited, especially as John now has four grandsons to accommodate, as well as a new granddaughter.

We loved Australia and it ticked lots of boxes for us, however, apart from the financial implications, it would have meant not seeing our families as often as we liked. The USA would also have meant no language problems and was slightly closer than Australia, but again our pensions would not be index linked there. Having considered all our options we decided that the Mediterranean climate and European culture were what we were really looking for.

You will no doubt have your own priorities and may decide to look at more far-flung places, especially if you don't have family ties in the UK, but remember to use your head as well as your heart when contemplating where your dream home will be.

If you have never lived abroad it may be wise to rent somewhere in the area first, rather than burning your bridges, selling up in the UK, moving somewhere and finding out that the place you loved on your summer holidays is not the same in winter, and you miss the UK too much. If the only thing you miss is Marmite, however, then you can decide to make the move a permanent one, and get your relatives to bring over jars of the stuff whenever they visit you.

Having discovered the exorbitant price of decent tea bags when you buy them abroad, and as I cannot live without my morning cuppa, I will be insisting that visitors put a box in their cases before coming to visit us. Whatever your own must-have British food or drink, if you can't wait for your next visitors to arrive with their precious consignment, you can always order them on-line through various specialist websites, or look in "British supermarkets" – if you don't mind the prices.

While I was in the WRNS I was stationed in Gibraltar, so I had visited Spain frequently and made many Spanish friends. I still remember a young man buying me a drink in La Linea and being told by the barman that this was the well-known bullfighter, Paco Camino. Unfortunately my Spanish at that time only consisted of a few words, including the important "gracias", whilst Paco's English seemed to be limited to "Bobby Charlton very good" and other phrases connected to football! I remember thinking that was a shame, as he was a good-looking and charming man.

I also recollect being invited round to the home of some Spanish friends one evening. After our meal I was offered a peach brandy, which I had never tried before and which I enjoyed, although I did think that one was probably enough. After I had said how good it was though, our host insisted that I should have another one. To make things worse for me the hostess handed round a basket of sweets; I eagerly accepted one, but I found it rather sickly, especially after the liqueurs. Luckily they then served some strong coffee, which was far better for my palate. Although I have a sweet tooth, Spaniards seem to have an even sweeter one, so I am now more careful when trying out Spanish foods and drinks.

Having experienced Spanish hospitality and generosity when I was in my twenties, Spain was an obvious choice for my shortlist of favourite places for retirement. I knew how friendly and welcoming the people are, and having spent many holidays there in more recent years nothing had occurred to change my opinion.

Before we met, John had only visited Spain once. Although he had been staying in Barcelona he had explored the surrounding area, and had also gone to Figueres for the day.

"I liked the Spanish people plus the food, and in particular the wine, went down well!" was his comment when we were discussing where we would like to retire to, and I had suggested Spain. "Northern Spain reminds me of the south of France, which obviously I know a lot better, having stayed with my ex's mother on numerous occasions. Maybe we could go there on holiday and see whether we both like the country enough to retire there?" I was happy with this suggestion, as I don't need much of an excuse to go on holiday.

So Spain was a frontrunner at this stage but we were still considering other options in Europe. We were also tempted by the south of France, where John and I have been on many holidays together and where we also enjoyed the way of life. France would have been easier in some respects, as we both speak a fair bit of French, however I was hoping to work as a complementary therapist, which ultimately ruled it out. The law in France prevents you from working as a complementary therapist unless you are medically qualified and, as you can imagine, I didn't fancy undertaking medical training at my advanced age. So forget Peter Mayle and his *Year in Provence* – we didn't particularly want to be his neighbours anyway – we decided that we were heading for Spain.

Implications Of Working Abroad

John and I are going to be retiring to Spain, so we are in the fortunate position of not having to work, though we both want to do more than just sit in the sun. If you need to find work in your new country do look into it thoroughly before deciding to move. Even being self-employed has implications, as I have only recently found out. I will need to make social security payments of over 200 euros every month, even if I am not making any money, so further investigation will be needed before I can set up my own business, especially as I only want to do it on a part-time basis. I may need to try and find employment working for somebody else, however unless I am living in an ex-pat community I will need to improve my Spanish first.

When I first looked into the possibility of working as a therapist abroad I couldn't find any UK based insurance companies who would cover me if I was living in Spain. Many therapists still reside in the UK and only work in Spain for a few months every year, so they don't have a problem. Luckily my current insurers are now going to extend their cover to therapists who are permanently based in Spain, so that is one potential problem resolved.

I will also need a licence from the local town hall, though I have been assured that this will only be a nominal fee. I am still trying to find out as much information as possible before setting myself up in business and would advise anybody else who intends working for themselves to do their homework too before moving.

If you are hoping to work for somebody else there are several factors to consider. Do you speak fluent Spanish? If not, that will limit you to working with ex-pats and you are likely to be in competition with other Brits looking for similar jobs. Do you have skills that are in demand in the area that you will be moving to? Have you checked how much money you are likely to be paid in Spain? Your wages will be lower than in the UK, so once you have found a job you need to know that you will be able to survive on less money. Of course many things are cheaper in Spain, so it's not all doom and gloom. The general advice to anybody moving to another country and hoping to find work there is to have at least one year's living expenses in your bank account to cover you until you are settled and in work earning money.

Narrowing The Field

Many people choose Spain because of the climate, but don't necessarily like Spanish food or particularly want to mix with the local people, which is why there are so many large ex-pat communities. If that's what you want, then go for it, but we decided we would prefer to live in a more traditional Spanish town.

Now we had identified which country we wanted to live in, but we still had to decide whether we would rather live on the coast or inland, and which area of Spain we wanted to settle down in. Spain of course is a vast country and, although we had visited many cities and regions including most of the Costas, we weren't sure exactly where we wanted to move to, so that's how we got onto the viewing trips merry-go-round.

CHAPTER TWO

To View Or Not To View?

The idea of a viewing trip is that you pay a small amount of money to an agency, which then books your hotel for you and helps to cover the cost of your flights. Usually they charge you a nominal sum (normally less than £99), so you may see this as a cheap holiday. If so, think again. You won't have much time to relax as the purpose of this trip is to find you a new home in the sun, which obviously means spending most of your time actually looking at houses rather than working on your tan.

When you arrive in Spain you will be met at the airport and driven to the hotel to drop off your luggage. Your agent will then take you around various new developments and in some cases may show you property re-sales. Some agencies escort prospective buyers in a group, which means that you could end up seeing properties which are out of your price range or in an area that you aren't interested in. We were more fortunate, as for each viewing trip that we have been on we had one person taking the two of us around (with one notable exception, which I will tell you about later). Personal service however did not make it any easier to find our dream home.

Decide Your Criteria

Our first viewing trips were to the Costa del Sol. We met several companies at various property shows in London, and had made it clear that we were on a limited budget, that we would need to sell our flat in London to finance our move, and the most important factor: we didn't want to stretch our budget too far. However this did not stop them from showing us properties well outside our price range.

Price was not the only issue for us. Unusually, neither of us drives because living in London we didn't need to do so. Of course one or both of us could learn, however we were going to be in our late fifties, if not older, when we moved to Spain, and being realistic, we were probably going to reach a stage where we would have to give up driving, even if we managed to pass the test now. It made sense to us to look for an area where public transport is good and we wouldn't need to have a car. Even if you are a driver you should think about the possibility of not being able to drive anymore when you get a lot older, and consider whether you would then want the upheaval of moving to a new home which is more accessible. I do wonder about elderly people who decide to live somewhere beautiful but remote: have they really thought it through? What will they do if they are no longer able to drive? How will they cope when their health starts to deteriorate, as inevitably it will?

The obvious solution would be to move to a Spanish city, however we didn't want to do this, partly because prices were likely to be higher and also, having lived in a large city for many years, we were looking for a more peaceful lifestyle. On the other hand, we did want to have a good-sized town nearby with a choice of shops, bars and restaurants. Like many people, we wanted the best of both worlds. You only have to watch TV programmes such as *A Place in the Sun* to see how demanding people can be, and John and I were not the exceptions.

Because I was hoping to continue working as a complementary therapist, and John also wanted an opportunity to work part-time, we made it clear that we wanted to look at developments that were a reasonable size, preferably with sporting facilities. This was partly because we enjoy sport and partly because injured sports people would be potential clients for me. We didn't really want to be on the coast, though, in a typical ex-pat community, as we thought we would get more for our money inland, plus we wanted to experience the "real" Spain.

Another reason to avoid the coast was that I had lived in a seaside town in Lincolnshire for several years and was aware how different life can be in winter compared to the lively resort visitors see in summer months. In my case, though, I had preferred living there out of season, where I enjoyed the feeling of being part of a close local community. As our household income wasn't dependent on holidaymakers I didn't appreciate having them around in summer, especially when they tossed their rubbish into our front garden. Having a young family and not much money at that time, I had also resented the inevitable increases in prices during the summer months.

Luckily John agreed with my sentiments, so we told the agent that an inland property was what we were looking for. Unfortunately we discovered that some agents think that when you say "inland", what you mean is a five-minute drive from the coast and a property on an ex-pat development.

In our naivety we assumed that having given the agents our budget and having made our requirements clear (inland, a fairly big development with sporting facilities, good public transport, and near a large typically Spanish town), it would be easy to find our new home. We soon learnt otherwise.

First Viewing Trip

Our first viewing trip was to the Costa del Sol, even though we had reservations about our budget being large enough. One of the first places we were shown was within our budget – just – but it was very hard to judge whether it was going to be value for money, as we stood on top of a hilltop looking at a large plot of land with a tape round it. Was this it? Apparently it was. Welcome to the world of off-plan developments.

I eventually managed to speak (John was still looking around, speechless for once, slowly shaking his head). "Is there a show home to give us some idea of what the houses will be like?" I asked the agent, Magda. The answer was no, although she said that we could look at the plans and the drawings of the proposed development. By now John was muttering under his breath: "She cannot be serious!"

I have a good imagination, but this was taking it a bit too far. It might have been different if we were only looking for an investment; however this was going to be our future home. I needed to see a house, walk around it and imagine myself living there. I could appreciate the views from that hilltop, but I needed more than a view to persuade me that this was the place to buy.

On the way back to our hotel Magda realised that she hadn't quite sold the idea to us, so with great enthusiasm she told us about the large German community living there already and the good local German schools. Now please don't get me wrong, I have some lovely German friends, but at the time we were a couple in our fifties, so was it likely that we would be interested in good local schools, whether they were German, British or Spanish? Obviously it was not going to be a selling point as far as we were concerned.

All was not lost however, according to Magda. She had another development to take us to and this time we could look at an actual house. We went there and saw the show home, which was a good-sized house that we liked the look of, however we also realised that it was a long way to the nearest town. Although we are keen walkers, the walk there was downhill, which obviously meant the walk back would be uphill!

"I wouldn't fancy carrying the shopping back up that hill!" John commented. We also made the point that although we might be very fit now we would be retiring to Spain and inevitably over the years we would become less able to walk long distances.

We went back to the UK without parting with our money, which was fortunate as we later discovered that the developers did not have any licences to build in the areas we had been looking at. Apparently many developers do start building while waiting for permission, and you have probably read horror stories about ex-pats having problems with illegal builds, so don't part with any money until your solicitor has confirmed that licences are in place and you have your bank guarantee. More about that later – as we found out, you cannot assume that the buying process in Spain is similar to the British system.

Wasting Our Time

Our next visit to the Costa del Sol was also a waste of time from our point of view. Many of the properties were way above our upper limit, so we made it clear to the agent that we were not willing to go over our budget. Bill listened carefully and promised us that he had a development to show us that he thought we would love and he said that this time the price was right.

First impressions were good: it was a golf development that was close to completion and we liked the setting. We were slightly disappointed, although not surprised, to find out that the only property we could afford was an apartment within a large block. It was a decent size though and very nice inside. It might have been a contender, apart from one factor: it was too far from the nearest town and there were no buses. Bill clearly had a good sense of humour, as he suggested we could use a golf buggy to get to the shops. We went back home again with our deposit money still untouched.

We had suspected from the beginning that the Costa del Sol was a non-starter and we agreed that we would not be persuaded by any overly keen salesmen at London property shows to go there again. Prices were too high, plus there were too many ex-pat communities when what we were looking for was something completely different. We wanted to live in a real Spanish community, away from British pubs and restaurants serving Sunday roasts. So the next viewing trip was to be to Almería, an area we hadn't visited before. We could hardly wait.

Getting Warmer

This was more like it. We were really excited on the drive from Almería airport to Mojacar, as the landscape was stunning and the villages we went through were lovely. We had to hide our smiles when we stopped for a late lunch with Mike, our agent, and realised that although he had been living in the area for several years his Spanish wasn't as good as ours. This is a serious point though, as if you are going to look at properties in Spanish communities, as we were doing, surely your agent should be able to communicate properly with the local people? Some of the staff at the sites we visited hardly spoke any English, so it would have been helpful if our agent could have asked them questions on our behalf in Spanish.

However Mike did make a very good suggestion to us before we went for our first viewing. He said that we should both give marks out of ten for every property we looked at and he would write those down. Towards the end of our trip we could then see if there was one place that we had both rated highly and if so, we could go back for another look. Whether you look round with an agent or independently, it is a good idea to do this.

Buying a property abroad, whether it is to be a holiday home or your permanent residence, is a gigantic step, and if you are in a relationship you both need to be totally committed to it. As John is easy-going I didn't want him to agree with what he knew I wanted unless he too really loved the place. I encouraged him to rate properties first - as I certainly wouldn't give a high rating to somewhere just because John liked it - so that way I would know whether he really was as keen as I was.

We learnt a lot more about what we wanted from that particular viewing trip. We saw lots of properties that we loved, however they were in the wrong location for various reasons: too remote, too close to the motorway, too quiet or too noisy. We also found many places where we could have lived quite happily, however the houses were too small or too expensive, or just too ugly for us to consider living there. It became clear to us that it wasn't going to be as easy as we thought to find our ideal place in the sun.

Ask The Right Questions

We discovered the importance of asking the right questions. One development really appealed to us: the houses were well designed and very attractive, plus they were reasonably priced and spacious inside. We were very tempted although the nearby village was quite small, which meant that we would need to travel to the nearest large town to find a supermarket and other shops, plus restaurants if we fancied a night out. Mike told us there was a bus service to the town, which sounded promising. We were in the sales office when I decided to ask the salesman there about the bus service. "It runs regularly during the summer months," we were told. "What about the winter months?" I asked, prepared to be told it wasn't as frequent. "There aren't any buses in winter," was the reply. Next!

Once again we flew back to the UK without finding our dream home, although we both agreed that we preferred Almería to the Costa del Sol.

"The Costa del Sol is fine for holidays – so long as we go out of season when the hordes aren't there – but when it comes to living somewhere all year round I much prefer Almería!" was John's opinion, and I had to agree with him.

Sue Walker

CHAPTER THREE

We're All Going On
A Summer Holiday

John and I decided that, purely in the name of research, we needed to investigate other regions in Spain. John spread out his map of Spain on our dining table and, as we studied it, we realised how many places we had never visited, and that there was a lot more to see than the Costa del Sol and Costa Blanca. In theory we could have spent the next 10 years at least exploring this fascinating country trying to find our ideal spot, but we wanted to buy somewhere for holidays and to eventually retire to, so we needed to start our research immediately. Any excuse for a holiday!

A Coruña

Unlike Cliff Richard in the film "Summer Holiday" we didn't travel on a London bus, however we did go on a lot of planes, trains and local Spanish buses in the course of our investigations.

"Let's start in the north and work our way towards the south," John suggested. "After all we have already visited the Costa del Sol and decided it isn't for us. We can go on the internet to book our flights and accommodation."

"I shouldn't have any problems getting leave so long as I give enough notice," I told him. "What about going in May? It should be lovely and sunny then."

We decided to stay just outside A Coruña (or La Coruña as it is known in Spanish) in Galicia, a province we had never visited before. The week before we were due to arrive we had a phone call from the manager of the hotel asking whether we needed an airport pick-up. "It's raining at the moment, but the forecast looks good for next week," he assured us. Rain! I thought this was meant to be sunny Spain.

Luckily the forecast was accurate and we had a week of lovely warm weather, but we realised why part of the northern coast is known as the Costa Verde, or Green Coast. Northern Spain does get a lot more rain than other parts of the country, which is why there is so much greenery around. Our dream home had to be in the sun, so although we enjoyed our holiday this was probably not the place for us.

I had an interesting experience when we were in Galicia. I decided that my hair was getting a bit untidy and I really needed a trim. I walked into a small hairdressing salon near where we were staying and spoke in my limited Castilian Spanish (Castellano) to a male hairdresser, who booked me an appointment for the following day. When I turned up in the morning he wasn't there, however there was a very friendly female hairdresser who hardly spoke any Castilian Spanish and, as my knowledge of Galician (Galego) is practically nil, we had a lot of fun communicating with each other.

Two old ladies were sitting waiting for their turn, but insisted that I went first. I suspect I was providing them with free entertainment as the hairdresser and I tried to work out what I wanted her to do. She kept saying "más" whereas I insisted, "No. Solo un poco," with much waving of hands and laughter all round. To my amazement I eventually walked out with the haircut that I wanted and of course it was far cheaper than back home in London, which was a bonus. John also had his hair cut, though the process was much simpler as he didn't mind how much of his hair was cut off, so the entertainment he provided wasn't as good.

We decided to show off our new haircuts in A Coruña, as we had discovered that there was a bus stop near the hotel where we could catch a bus into the city, and we needed to check whether we could get back to the airport under our own steam.

The bus was crowded and we soon discovered why as later on we stood watching a big military parade. Troops marched along the sea front, the King and Queen drove by waving to the cheering crowds, the navy performed their manoeuvres out at sea and there was an impressive fly past at the end.

Half way through the ceremony we noticed that there was a gap in the procession. Suddenly we heard a mobile phone ring.

"Look over there!" John nudged me and pointed to where a solitary policeman stood on the opposite side of the street. The rather sheepish-looking police officer was answering his phone and when the crowd realised what was happening, somebody started clapping. Soon everybody was laughing and clapping as the unfortunate policeman walked hurriedly down the road. We were discovering that Spaniards have a good sense of humour and always enjoy having a laugh.

We reached the conclusion that we would return to Galicia for a holiday, but that we would not be looking there for our new home, partly because this was not the sunny Spain that we wanted to live in but also because of potential language problems. Our command of Castilian Spanish wasn't that good, but to learn Galego would be even more difficult. We still had many other areas to consider though, so from my point of view I had lots more holidays to look forward to.

Almería Revisited

We had already visited Costa Almería and liked the region, so although we had some reservations about whether it was suitable for us as non-drivers, we decided to book an apartment at Vera Playa for a holiday, which would give us a chance to assess the area independently.

"If we can get around OK on holiday then it might be worth looking at properties there again," John suggested.

"Well we didn't get much chance to explore on our own did we? I would love to have an actual holiday there." Luckily we both got a generous holiday entitlement where we worked.

Our reasons for investigating Costa Almería further were partly because prices were considerably lower than on the Costa del Sol and partly because we thought it was more like the Spain we were looking for, with dramatic scenery, lots of history and not over developed.

As well as renting an apartment in Vera Playa for a week we also booked a hotel in Almería for a couple of nights.

Almería is a charming city steeped in history and we enjoyed exploring it, though we weren't seriously considering buying there as we wanted a change from city life. Almería is located at the foot of a mountain range which is crowned by the magnificent Alcazaba. The Alcazaba is amazing and well worth the steep climb to reach it, though I would avoid going there if you don't like cats, as there were more of them wandering around it than I have ever seen in one place.

"I can't see any mice around here, can you?" John commented.

What we also liked about Almería was that there are so many lovely winding old streets to wander along, while stopping occasionally for a rest and to enjoy a drink and tapas. Many of the bars in the back streets follow the old tradition of serving free tapas with your drink, which was an added bonus for low-budget travellers like us.

Vera Playa is a pleasant resort on the Almerían coast, and we found that there were plenty of apartments for sale there, however as already stated we didn't want to live close to the sea. If you don't mind paying more for the pleasure of being on the coast and don't mind the crowds during the summer months, you will find that prices are more reasonable than in many other coastal regions, so it could be worth considering.

Mojacar is a typical "Pueblo Blanco" (the many villages in Andalusia with white-washed houses are popularly known as "White Villages"): very quaint and inevitably popular with tourists. We were there off-season and I dread to think how crowded it gets in the summer months as there were already lots of other visitors wandering around. The views are amazing and we had to fight for space on the village terrace to take our photos. We managed to get away from the maddening crowds by walking uphill and, although it was hard work as it was very steep, we were rewarded when we found a lovely bar with a smaller terrace at the top of the village, where only a few locals were having a drink. Luckily, they didn't seem to mind sharing the view with us.

We witnessed a spectacular event in Mojacar Pueblo, where horsemen charged down the street with what appeared to be pencils in their hands. No doubt they would have been carrying lances not that many years ago! We arrived in Mojacar in time to witness all the drama. A row of señoritas wearing beautiful traditional dresses and of varying ages and sizes had lined up on a balcony overlooking the street. Down below, gallant horsemen took it in turns to charge past them, with their "lance" in one hand and attempted to spear one of the bright ribbons that had been hung on a line across the street.

If they were successful they reined in their horse, dismounted and went to present the ribbon to the señorita of their choice. To do this they had to clamber up a stepladder until they were level with the balcony and were then rewarded by being able to kiss the hand, or the cheek, of their chosen señorita as they handed her their ribbon. It did occur to me that it would have been more romantic if the señoritas had let down their hair for the señor to climb up, or perhaps lowered a rope, rather than using a mundane stepladder.

"Watch out!" John suddenly grabbed my arm. He had noticed that a particularly large and lively horse had decided to back into the crowd.

Everybody moved out of its way quickly and one small child started crying, however a couple of minutes later the horse was under control so people moved forward again. I must admit that I didn't bother to fight my way back to the front, having seen the size of the next horse riding towards us.

We were on our way down the hill after exploring Mojacar Pueblo, when we decided to have a drink in a café on one of the many lovely plazas. The waiter brought our drinks over and indicated that we should have a look at the tapas on the counter.

"I don't know about you, but I'm a bit peckish," John said to me.

"Well we didn't intend staying so long, but we couldn't miss watching the horse display, could we? Let's see what tapas they've got." I was the first to go and check them out, hoping they wouldn't all be meat ones as I was definitely getting hungry.

There was a good selection, so I chose prawns while John had difficulty in deciding but eventually settled for one of the meat dishes.

The waiter brought over a plate which had three huge gambas on it for me and John's meat had been put inside a small roll, looking like a miniature burger. When we received the bill we were amazed to find that such substantial tapas had not been charged for, especially when considering that we had been able to choose what we wanted. Usually, when you are given free tapas with your drink, it consists of a bowl of olives, nuts or crisps, or whatever the waiter has decided to give you. It was also an unexpected gesture as Mojacar is such a popular tourist spot.

We enjoyed walking round Garrucha too. It is a Spanish fishing village just north of Mojacar Playa, where fish is obviously the best choice in the local restaurants, which of course suited me. If we were to change our minds and live on the coast our preference would be a working town like Garrucha rather than a resort like Vera or Mojacar.

We decided to dine out at one of the fish restaurants there. When we entered the restaurant the waiter came over and spoke to us in very good English. On the coast most restaurant and bar staff are pretty fluent, which is fortunate for the many holiday-makers who don't speak a word of Spanish.

The menus we were given were in English, and we couldn't recognise many of the dishes because of the slightly bizarre translations. We called the waiter over and asked him, in Spanish, if we could have the Spanish menu. He obliged and then spoke to us in Spanish for the rest of the evening.

We discovered that the town of Vera is 10km inland and the bus ride from Vera Playa took about half an hour as it seemed to visit every development in the area, but it was certainly worth a visit. There is plenty to see there, including a bullring with a museum where you can dress up as a matador if you are that way inclined (John was, and I have the photo to prove it). Another strenuous uphill walk to another monument on a hill, with the sun beating down on us, may have been hard, sweaty work, but again the views made it worthwhile. We liked the town but it was a bit smaller than we ideally wanted and we discovered that many places shut during the siesta, including some bars and restaurants, so it was difficult even finding somewhere to have lunch.

Enjoy A Fiesta

Fiestas are often held in celebration of a local saint and many of them will have strong religious overtones. We watched a procession in Vera where the statue of Christ was carried solemnly through the streets of the town by a small group of men dressed in traditional thick costumes that looked as if they would have been hot to wear on such a sunny day. We followed the procession as they walked slowly around the town on what must have been an exhausting journey, dressed as they were and carrying what was obviously a very heavy statue.

After they had eventually returned the statue to the church the celebrations began and we listened to the bands playing in the square for a while, before looking for somewhere to eat. Most of the restaurants had set up bars outside where they were serving food and drinks to the revellers, so we enjoyed an alfresco meal at one of them before heading for the bus back to the coast.

We needed to catch two buses into Almería the day before we were due to fly back to the UK. The bus from Vera was late arriving at Vera Playa, even though it was the first bus of the day so we had expected it to be on time. We were becoming a bit anxious, however when we arrived at the stop in Garrucha we could see other people waiting there. Obviously the second bus was also late so we hadn't missed it.

We know that bus drivers won't sell you a ticket when you are at a bus station as they expect you to buy one before you board the bus, however this stop was in a village, so we assumed that we could get tickets from the driver. This was how we found out that, even if there isn't a bus station nearby, there may be a local shop where you are expected to purchase your ticket before the bus arrives.

Luckily John is very observant and while we were waiting for the connecting bus in Garrucha he spotted a couple of men holding tickets. We asked where they had bought them and John just had time to dash to the shop before the bus turned up.

The journey back to Almería took a lot longer than our original bus ride to Vera Playa. As the driver opted for the scenic route through the desert area where many Spaghetti Westerns have been filmed, we enjoyed the journey. Further delays were caused when we drove through a small town that must have been celebrating a local fiesta as there was a long, slow procession of floats also going through it. We didn't complain though as it was a colourful display and we were beginning to realise that in Spain processions and fiestas always have priority. I must admit that we might not have been as patient if we had been catching our flight the same day.

What we liked about the region of Almería: the stunning scenery, lovely Spanish towns and reasonable prices. Why we decided not to buy there: for non-drivers the infrastructure is not as well developed as elsewhere. If we had missed the bus from Garrucha to Almería, we would have had a long wait as there were only a couple of buses a day.

Almería was another part of Spain to add to our list of places to visit on holiday and may very well be a suitable area for you to consider when looking for your permanent home, however as far as we were concerned it did not have enough facilities, so our search for our new home in the sun continued.

Sue Walker

CHAPTER FOUR

It's Party Time

One of the many highlights of our frequent visits to Spain has been experiencing local fiestas. Sometimes we have deliberately gone on holiday to a particular place at a particular time because we have been aware that there was going to be a fiesta while we were staying there, but at other times we have been lucky enough to stumble on a celebration which we hadn't known about in advance, like the one we had witnessed in Mojacar.

The following year John had an important birthday to celebrate and we decided to return to a city that we had really loved the first time we went there: Valencia. We had always vowed to go back again to see the sights that we had missed on our first visit and this seemed an appropriate time to do so.

The celebrations started in London on John's actual birthday and a few weeks' later we flew to Valencia with some friends to continue partying during "Las Fallas", one of Spain's most spectacular fiestas. We had read about Las Fallas (the Fires), which takes place every March with a riotous week of fires, explosions and parades in honour of San José (St. Joseph).

"What better way to celebrate your 60th birthday?" I asked John.

"Are you paying?" he said hopefully.

"You won't get any other presents if I do!" was my response, as I took out my credit card. "I can take a hint though."

If you have never been to Valencia for Las Fallas I would highly recommend it, unless of course you are of a nervous disposition. Read on and you will soon find out why.

Valencia – Las Fallas

The local districts within the city build their own "ninots": vast colourful papier-mâché figures, which can be fifteen to twenty feet high. These are usually satirical, either sending up local celebrities or people who are well-known worldwide, especially politicians. The year we went we particularly liked the figure of Tony Blair, shown as a puppet with George Bush holding his strings.

The districts will also have smaller, brightly coloured statues, like cartoon characters, for the children to enjoy. Our friends' daughter Juliette liked looking at these, especially the characters that she recognised.

Throughout the week fireworks were being set off all over the city, however the highlight was the daily "mascletá", which took place in the Plaza Ayuntamiento at 2pm: a mass of fireworks, explosions, rockets and firecrackers. The whole ground seemed to tremble, as if there had been a massive earthquake. This is definitely not suitable for those of a nervous disposition. We also witnessed several processions, with smartly dressed, smiling children parading in their traditional costumes, watched by their proud families.

On the last night only one of the ninots is saved, after there has been a vote to select the favourite, which is then preserved in the Museum of the Ninots, while the rest of them are burnt. Months of hard work disappear in minutes, but as soon as Las Fallas finishes the neighbourhoods start planning for next year's fun and fireworks.

John and I were walking back to the hotel with our friend Cathy just before midnight on what was to be our last night in Valencia. We had enjoyed dinner with our other friends earlier, but Juliette was sleepy so they had taken her back to their hotel.

The restaurant where we had dined didn't have anything suitable for Juliette on their menu, however that had not been a problem as this was Spain. The friendly waiter had been far more interested in finding something for the child to eat than worrying about the adults. He had proudly presented Juliette with a plate of chicken breast and other food that he had been told the little girl would enjoy. Only after Juliette had started tucking into her meal had he seemed happy to give his full attention to the rest of the group. In Spain nothing is too much trouble where children are concerned.

As we were passing one of the local bars John suggested having a coffee. Although he didn't say so, I knew him well enough to know that probably meant a brandy too.

"Not for me, I'm feeling tired, and we need to be up early in the morning," Cathy said. She decided to continue to the hotel, which was only a short walk away.

I was sitting on a stool at the bar enjoying a cup of café solo (small black coffee) with a splash of brandy from John's glass, when he decided to take a look through the back door, which was half open.

"Come here and see what's happening outside", he commanded. "There's a huge bonfire in the square behind the bar."

We walked out to have a closer look and realised that they were about to burn the giant ninots. A couple of men were climbing up ladders to reach the top of each one and set fire to it. As huge flames leapt into the sky we watched the models gradually crumple and disintegrate into cinders.

As we turned to go back into the bar we noticed a large marquee that had been erected in the square and, being inquisitive, I decided to take a look inside. There was a stage at the far end where a band had started tuning up and a bar had been set up in the corner. Other people started drifting in and they invited us to join them. Soon the party was in full swing, with people of all ages dancing and having a good time. Although they knew we weren't locals we were made to feel very welcome. We practised our Spanish on them and they practised their English on us, with a lot of laughter and smiles.

Three hours later, having danced until we were exhausted, we left the locals to continue with their festivities and walked wearily back to our hotel. Cathy was surprised to see how tired we were at breakfast, until we told her about the party we had joined and which she had unfortunately missed.

Valencia is one of our favourite Spanish cities, however we knew that we wouldn't be looking at buying a home there, although no doubt we will return for more holidays in future years. The search would have to continue elsewhere.

The Basque Country

John and I had entered the World Masters Track and Field Championships that year. These are held every two years in different countries and this time they were taking place in San Sebastián in northern Spain. We had competed in the Championships a couple of times previously: once in the UK and once in Australia. This would be an ideal opportunity to go to the Basque country, which we had never visited before.

John is a much better athlete than I am and does well in his event, the 2000m steeplechase. Luckily they allow athletes of all standards to compete in different age groups, so I had decided to enter the 100m and 200m sprints. I enjoy sprinting, as even if I come last there is no danger of better athletes lapping me!

We decided to stay in Bilbao, as the cheaper hotels in San Sebastián had already been booked well in advance. We would get the bus from Bilbao and stay a couple of nights in San Sebastián on the days when we were both competing; however we would spend the rest of our holiday in Bilbao.

It's reassuring to know that you can get a meal late at night when you are arriving in Spain on an evening flight from the UK. We were a bit concerned that our flight might be delayed and that by the time we reached the hotel we could miss dinner. We sent an email to our hotel explaining this and asked them when they stopped serving meals. Their answer came back saying that dinner was available until 11pm, so not to worry.

Luckily the flight arrived on schedule, so we had time to check in and have a quick shower before going down to the dining room at quarter to eleven. The place was still busy though we didn't hear any English voices, so presumably our fellow countrymen had dined a lot earlier. We noticed that couples were still arriving for dinner up until midnight and nobody was turned away. I'm not sure whether that would have happened back home in London.

Afterwards we decided to go for a stroll as we had eaten well and didn't want to go straight to bed on a full stomach. We discovered that this was the last day of a local fiesta, so there were bands playing and food being cooked at stalls all along the river, although sadly we were too full to sample any of the delicious smelling food.

Groups of young people were sitting on the pavement, sharing bottles of wine and other bottles of alcohol, chatting noisily with much laughter, but generally well-behaved with no signs of being drunk. It was a pleasant change from late nights we have experienced in cities back in the UK, but typical of Spain.

Enjoying Yet Another Fiesta

We had checked the internet before we left to see if there would be any other fiestas in the area while we were staying in Bilbao. We discovered that the pretty fishing village of Lekeitio was going to be holding one so we added it to our list of places to visit.

The bus to Lekeitio was packed, so obviously this was a popular event. We could see that it was going to take place mainly around the sea front, so we decided to explore the rest of the village first before heading with the masses towards the harbour.

Lekeitio is a combination of traditional Basque mansions, fishermen's houses and Gothic architectural gems such as the church of Santa María de la Asunción. There are two lovely beaches overlooking the island of San Nicolás however John and I, with our love of clambering up steep hills, decided to head for the highest point of the village rather than going for a casual stroll along the beach. There we were rewarded with magnificent views of the whole village, including the beaches and the harbour, which we could see was now packed with small boats.

We loved the whole carnival atmosphere when we eventually went down to the harbour: music was being played and both young children and old grannies were dancing in the street. The main event though was rather gruesome from a British viewpoint. We spotted a goose hanging from a rope strung across the middle of the harbour and we soon found out why it was there. Before I continue I would like to reassure you that the geese being used were all dead, although we suspect that in the past it might have been different.

We could see dozens of boats bobbing up and down in the harbour, as the crews waited their turn. Each team rowed towards the middle of the harbour with one person standing in the stern of the boat. The person at the back grabbed hold of the goose as the boat reached it and, as they did so, half a dozen strong men at the other end of the rope raced along the harbour side so that the goose swung high into the air, with somebody hanging on to its neck. The men holding the rope raced backwards and forwards, so the goose alternated between swinging high in the air and plunging towards the water, until either its neck broke or the person clinging onto it had fallen into the sea.

Whilst all this was going on young men and women were jumping into the harbour fully clothed and then swimming out to join the boats. I noticed a man swimming with one hand up in the air and realised, when he clambered aboard the boat, that he had been holding his cigarettes and matches. Many of the boats were being loaded with crates of beer and bottles of wine, so obviously there was going to be a lot of partying later on.

After every team had taken its turn there was a final race around the island between all the successful teams. No doubt the party would be continuing until the small hours, however John and I had to make sure we caught the last bus back to Bilbao.

I have to say that we had very mixed feelings about our experiences that day. The carnival atmosphere had been great fun and we had enjoyed watching the boats racing round the island. The local people were welcoming and were very friendly towards the strangers in their midst. We had a good time exploring what we imagined would be a rather quiet fishing village in normal circumstances and we would be happy to go there again. The only negative side was witnessing what seemed to our eyes to be a rather barbaric spectacle, and we can only hope that one day the dead geese will be replaced by something symbolic.

We have never been to a bullfight and have no intention of doing so, even though we can appreciate that it would be a colourful and dramatic spectacle. We have looked around bullrings and visited their museums, so we can understand the history behind bull fighting and admire the bravery of the matadors, but it's not something we want to support.

However I do feel that we are not in a position to criticise the Spanish love of bullfighting and similar traditions when you consider that, until recent years, it was acceptable in the UK for groups of riders and hounds to chase foxes and watch them being torn to pieces. This of course is my personal, not exactly objective, opinion.

We love most Spanish traditions, and know that many fiestas have been going on for centuries, however some of them are now being adapted to suit modern sensibilities and are becoming more safety conscious.

We had noticed that hundreds of firemen were on standby during Las Fallas when we were in Valencia, and ambulances were also ready in case of injuries - or possibly people fainting from sheer excitement! We knew that we could look forward to enjoying many more fiestas once we found our home in Spain, and we would highly recommend checking for local fiestas before holidaying there, as they enhance the whole Spanish experience. As we had already discovered, Spanish people love to party and they are more than happy to accept strangers in their midst.

Although we were there to compete in San Sebastián, we found time to explore the town too, and this time we discovered two steep hills to climb up, giving us amazing views of the lovely shell-shaped bay that San Sebastián is renowned for. On our way to climb the second hill we heard the sound of music so decided to find out what was happening. We walked towards the plaza where the music was coming from and could see lots of stands set up there, and people sampling cider.

"We can come back here after our walk," I insisted, before John could head towards the action. "You will have worked up quite a thirst by then."

Luckily for John the cider festival was still in full flow when we returned after our strenuous walk, and I have to admit that I was pretty thirsty by then, so enjoyed sampling the cider as much as he did. We were told that we could buy a glass for five euros and after that all the tastings were free. We wandered around the different stands, where they held the cider bottle high in the air before aiming it at our glasses, in most cases with great accuracy.

After we came back from our last holiday we decided that it was time to continue our search for a new home in Spain. We had already crossed a few places off our list of potential areas, including the Costa del Sol, northern Spain and Almería, but we still hadn't given up hope of finding somewhere suitable. The only question was, where should we look next?

Sue Walker

CHAPTER FIVE

We've Found Our Dream Home... Or Have We?

David, a manager with the UK Company that had arranged our trip to Almería, had phoned us after we got home to ask what we had thought about the trip. We were very honest: we said we had quite specific requirements and although the agent had taken us to lots of different developments, nothing we saw had met them all. We had liked Almería, but were unsure whether it would be the right area for us to live in permanently.

David asked John to go through our requirements again and listened very carefully to what he had to say.

"I think that the Costa Blanca might be a better bet for you," he said after John had gone into great detail about what we were looking for.

"We have already looked at the Costa Blanca," John said, slowly shaking his head as he looked at me, indicating that he didn't think this phone call was going to help us in our search. "Most of the properties were way over our budget and those that we could afford weren't in areas where we would want to live."

I waited impatiently, and with growing disbelief, as it appeared as if John was agreeing to go on yet another viewing trip that I knew would prove to be a waste of time.

"Well?" I demanded, when he eventually put down the phone.

"David seemed to take all my comments on board. He said that because the Costa Blanca is more established than Costa Almería, the infrastructure is more advanced and in particular the public transport system is good, however to get more for our money we should be looking inland."

"Exactly what we have been saying for the past couple of years!" I interrupted him, unable to believe that at long last somebody was actually suggesting to us that we should look inland.

"That is why I have agreed that we will go on one more viewing trip there. Now, we need to look at possible dates for when David gets back to me." John gave me a quick hug, before we checked our diaries to see when we would be able to fly to Spain again.

After so many wasted viewing trips we set off with low expectations, but high hopes. Would this trip turn out to be any different to our previous ones?

Guardamar Del Segura, Costa Blanca

This time we were not disappointed. We stayed at a hotel in Guardamar del Segura, which is situated on the southern Costa Blanca where the river Segura meets the sea. As far as we were concerned this was a good start to our trip, as Guardamar is a lovely unspoiled town, which helped to dispel our prejudices against places on the coast. As it was November we didn't expect it to be too crowded with holidaymakers though.

Guardamar is particularly popular with Spanish holidaymakers, although judging by the couple of English menus we spotted outside some Spanish restaurants when we strolled along the sea front before dinner, other nationalities are beginning to discover it. If you want to go for a less crowded walk a stroll past the sand dunes is very enjoyable and eventually you will reach the marina, which is certainly worth seeing. It was getting dark by the time we got there, but there was still enough light to appreciate how picturesque it was.

On our first night we were asked by Stella, the local estate agent who was showing us round, if we wanted to go to a Chinese restaurant, or maybe an Italian one? We looked at her in amazement and said, "Isn't there a Spanish restaurant we can go to?" To our relief she gave us a big smile and said that she knew a very good place, though it was a bit basic. Perfect – just what we wanted – good, simple Spanish food and good Spanish wine.

Although she was brought up in England Stella speaks Spanish fluently as her father is Spanish, which meant she was able to ask lots of questions on our behalf when we were dealing with Spanish developers and it inspired confidence in us. She was the ideal agent for us, as she listened carefully to what we wanted. The first few places we visited weren't quite what we were looking for, however they ticked a lot more boxes for us than other developments we had seen on our many previous viewing trips. At last, we felt somebody was really interested in what we wanted, and Stella seemed to be learning from our comments on the first properties she had shown us.

"I know that these aren't quite what you want, but by showing them to you I can understand better the type of property that suits you and what appeals to you in different areas," she explained. "Don't worry though; I won't be taking you anywhere that has lots of British bars and restaurants!"

"That's OK then," John told her. "Just make sure there is a good Spanish bar within walking distance and I'll be happy. There will have to be a couple of clothes shops for Sue though, to keep her quiet!"

Was This The One?

I can still clearly remember the day Stella first took us to see Residencial Santa Ana del Monte. She said, "This development is a long drive inland, but I believe that I have saved the best to last and that you will really like it, so I think it's worth going there." Luckily for her she was 100% right. I am not the best of travellers and that day I wasn't feeling very well, but as soon as we drove down to the site I made a miraculous recovery.

Forget sea views - give me a mountain view any day. The surroundings at Santa Ana del Monte are stunning, with mountain views in every direction and vineyards stretching from the development towards the local town of Jumilla. The show houses were impressive and when we looked round one of the Azucenas (two semi-detached houses backing onto another two, known in Spain as a quad) I could actually imagine myself living there.

"Would you like to look at the house again on your own?" Stella suggested, when we told her that we were interested in this particular property. "Take your time. I will have a chat with Pablo while you look around and you can come to the office when you are ready. We can then head into Jumilla for lunch."

This was the first property that we couldn't really find fault with. It was built in a traditional style, with a porch outside and there was a large living area with American style kitchen downstairs, plus a shower room. It was spacious enough for when we had visitors, but not too big for when we were on our own.

Upstairs there were two double bedrooms, one of which had a private balcony, plus a complete bathroom and the final touch was the solarium up on the roof.

"There is room here for a Jacuzzi," I said, only half joking, as we admired the views from the roof terrace.

"We would need to check whether the roof could take the weight." John as ever was being practical.

We walked down the stairs again, then through the master bedroom and onto the balcony. John put his arm round me as we looked over towards the mountains of Santa Ana del Monte.

"We could sit outside on the balcony after dinner with a glass of wine in our hands, watching the sun set over those mountains," he said. I for one could hardly wait!

"So, how many marks would you give this property?" I asked him, though I knew already by his reactions that he really liked the development. We both sensed that we had at long last found our ideal place in the sun.

"Probably nine marks. What about you?" This was a sign that John was definitely impressed by Residencial Santa Ana del Monte, as his previous highest mark had been seven for a property near Almería that he had been enthusiastic about, though unfortunately it had been a bit too remote for us.

"I will give it nine and a half. I don't believe that anywhere is going to be 100% perfect, but this is probably the closest we will get to our ideal property. Now, let's go and find Stella, as I'm getting hungry!"

Jumilla

Stella drove us into Jumilla for lunch and we found a local Spanish bar where we enjoyed a selection of tapas, a glass of vino tinto (red wine) for John and me, while Stella had to settle for a soft drink as she was the driver. We then had a stroll around the town before Stella asked us what we thought.

Jumilla is a lovely town, with some interesting old houses, many attractive squares and gardens, plenty of shops, cafes and bars, plus overlooking the town there is a fine 15th century Castle. As the nearest town to the new development, Jumilla seemed to have everything that we would need. In fact Jumilla was declared a city in 1911, though with a population of around 25,000, most people would consider it to be a town rather than a city.

"Stella, you were quite right. You definitely saved the best to last." Our search was over. After numerous interesting but ultimately frustrating viewing trips, it looked as if we had found our ideal place in the sun at Santa Ana del Monte.

John and I had already discussed what we wanted to do next. He had persuaded me not to hand over our money straight away, as this would be a major commitment for us. We needed to get to know the area better as you can only do so much on a viewing trip and we were due to fly back to the UK in a couple of days.

"We both like the property and we really love the surroundings, however we would like to come back to Jumilla on our own and have a good look around before finally making up our minds," John told Stella. "We will let you know when we have booked our flights. If we are still convinced it's the right place for us, we will contact you while we are over here and arrange to pay the reservation fee. Is that OK with you?"

"Of course it is. Let me know when you are going to arrive and if you want, either Mark or I will pick you up at the airport and drive you to wherever you are staying." Stella and her husband Mark worked together in the family estate agency. "Will you stay in Guardamar again? I know you like the hotel there."

"No. We will book a room at one of the hotels here in Jumilla, as the idea is to try out the local buses and find out whether we can get around easily, plus see what people in the town are like." I told Stella. "After all it was fine having lunch here today with you, but our Spanish is very basic, so it will be a chance to find out how we would cope on our own if we were living near a Spanish community."

"That makes sense. Now that I have shown you everything that I had found for you, and it looks as if you are happy with this final property, I will drive you back to your hotel and you can spend what's left of the day as you wish. If you don't mind having dinner with me later on, there is a lovely Spanish restaurant outside Guardamar that I want to show you. We can have a bit of a celebration!"

"Sounds like a good idea to me," John said. "After seeing Santa Ana del Monte, I think we are both in the mood for a celebration."

I nodded in agreement. I had begun to think, after so many hopeless viewing trips, that our dream of a new home in Spain was destined to stay as only a dream. It was lovely to have been proved wrong, and I knew that the first thing that we would do after returning to London would be to arrange for our return. That was definitely something to celebrate.

Getting A NIE

Stella advised us to apply for the all important Número de Identificación de Extranjeros (NIE number) while we were staying in Guardamar. This is basically a tax identification number and you must have one if you are going to reside and/or buy a property in Spain. We later discovered that you need your NIE number for almost everything that you do in Spain!

"You will have to get your NIE number at some stage, even if you change your mind about buying at Santa Ana del Monte," Stella told us. "Do you want me to speak to Sandra and see if she can arrange it before you go back?" Sandra was the English-speaking solicitor that we had found in Guardamar.

"OK. We've found somewhere now that we are interested in buying so it does make sense." We might not have agreed so readily though if we had known what time of day we would have to get up.

Sandra had arranged for us to be picked up at what seemed to us a ridiculously early hour, to ensure that we arrived at Elche police station early enough to be sure of being towards the front of the queue. Only a specific number of people will receive their NIE on a particular day so you have to be there early to guarantee that you will be one of them.

Stella's husband Mark picked us up from our hotel in Guardamar. We had negotiated with the restaurant manager at the hotel the night before so we were able to have a coffee and continental breakfast before they officially started serving breakfast. Mark dropped us off outside our solicitor's office in the middle of Guardamar at what still felt like the crack of dawn and we were met there by José, a clerk from the solicitors, who spoke a bit of English and had all the necessary papers for us to obtain our NIE numbers. We had already provided

Sandra with copies of our passports and had the originals with us.

We picked up another British couple en route. The husband George spoke good Spanish, so he sat in the front and chatted to José, but his wife Sheila told us that she didn't speak any Spanish and wasn't too bothered about learning. She said that George was more than capable of communicating in Spanish so there was no need for her to learn.

Sheila was a lovely lady, so I wasn't going to argue with her, but I couldn't really agree with this statement. She was going to be living in Spain too, so I felt that she should also learn some of the language and not have to rely on her husband. Their immediate neighbours were English; however Sheila would be missing the opportunity to get to know her other neighbours and to really get involved in and enjoy the Spanish way of life. However that was her choice, and I am sure there are many people like her, who are quite happy to live amongst other ex-pats. If you are one of them you need to be sure that you live somewhere where English is widely spoken, otherwise you risk feeling isolated.

José had picked George and Sheila up in La Marina, so I asked Sheila if they were living there. "No, we are buying a house in Urbanización – do you know it?" she asked. She was blissfully unaware how many towns are called "Urbanización" (urbanisation) in Spain, no doubt in part because she didn't know the language.

When we arrived at Elche, we could see why we had to have such an early pick-up as there were already quite a few people ahead of us. It was also fortunate that we were there early, as when José from the solicitor's office looked through our documents he told us that one of the photocopies wasn't clear enough, which potentially could have caused problems, so he disappeared to get a better copy.

At nine o'clock, they started calling people through and it wasn't long before it was our turn. The actual process was quite quick: they checked all our paperwork and then we were told to "sign here", which we did, and that was about it. The NIE numbers would be sent to our solicitor at a later date, so it was back to the car and the return journey to Guardamar, to make the most of the rest of our stay there.

Although the process of getting our NIE numbers was fairly painless, we know that other people have had worse experiences and our later dealings with Spanish bureaucracy proved to be a completely different story. One word of warning though: even if you read something in a specialist book about the way things happen in Spain things change all the time. I think the best advice I can give you is: when in Spain, be prepared for the unexpected.

Sue Walker

CHAPTER SIX

Making Our Minds Up!

W e were now convinced that we had found our ideal place in Spain; however it is very easy to get seduced when you are relaxing in the sun, drinking lots of good wine, with the love of your life – I'm sure that you know what I mean. You think you have found your perfect home abroad, but if this is going to be a permanent new home rather than just somewhere to spend your holidays, it is important not to rush into things too quickly.

Before you sign on the dotted line, hand over lots of money for your deposit and rush to sell your home in the UK, it is wise to step back and ask yourself if you are sure you know what you are doing. Renting in the area before actually buying a property there is advisable, but for many of us this is not a practical option. Visiting at different times of the year is also sensible, as some inland areas can be surprisingly chilly in winter, although if it is sunny it never seems as cold. My advice would be to stay in the area for a week or so at least before making your mind up. This is what John and I had decided to do, so we booked our flights to Alicante for the end of February and made a reservation for our hotel.

Be Really Sure

We arrived in Jumilla with great excitement and with 3,000 euros readily available for the reservation fee, as we had been advised by Stella. We had been told that if we made the decision to buy a house at Santa Ana del Monte, we would need to make a payment of 3,000 euros to secure the property of our choice for the next six weeks until contracts had been agreed and signed, at which stage we would have to pay the rest of the deposit.

We had already told Stella that we were definitely interested in buying the property at Residencial Santa Ana del Monte, but that we wanted to spend some time in the local town before finally committing ourselves, and she had agreed that it was sensible to do so.

The show house had impressed us, as it was a spacious, well-designed and attractive property. The surroundings were stunning with their lovely mountain views and the planned development would have everything that we wanted and more. This development was going to be a golf resort, but neither of us plays golf and we had no intention of becoming golfers. In our opinion, which we share with Mark Twain, golf is a good walk spoiled! We would make the most of some of the other sports facilities though, and living on a golf development meant that it would be busy all year round and not become a ghost town in the winter months.

As we don't drive we needed to know whether we could get around the area easily or whether we would find ourselves living in an isolated community. Would we cope living near a small Spanish town, with our limited language abilities? How would we be treated by the local people? We needed to have these questions answered before we could commit ourselves to such a major purchase.

I admit that we cheated a bit, as when we rang Stella to tell her that we had booked our flights and hotel, she said that Mark would pick us up at Alicante airport and drop us off at the Hotel Monreal in Jumilla, but once we arrived there we were on our own. The hotel receptionist spoke a little bit of English - about as much as our Spanish - so you have probably guessed by now that she wasn't exactly fluent. Smiles are an international language though, and it is amazing how well you can communicate with them along with a few words and some appropriate hand gestures.

Over the course of the week we were able to tick all the items on our checklist. We had decided that we wanted to try out lots of restaurants and bars, catch buses to other towns, go shopping and explore as much of Jumilla as possible. Top of the list though was finding out how friendly the local people were and the welcoming smile from the hotel receptionist was a good start.

Getting To Know The Place

We managed to try out nearly all of the restaurants and quite a few of the bars in Jumilla. We knew we wouldn't starve while we were there, as we can speak enough Spanish to ask for a menu, order our meal and drinks and pay the bill. Most restaurants only had menus in Spanish, which was fine, as when you get an English translation it doesn't always make sense and we already knew the names of many Spanish dishes. The prices were good - far cheaper than on the coast - and we found that most of the restaurant staff were very friendly. There was one exception (we called him Señor Grumpy) but maybe he had just had a bad day, so we won't name and shame him.

We went into a bar on one of the back streets for a drink one evening and wanted to have a couple of tapas with our wine, however we discovered that the tapas were all meat. Although I am not a vegetarian as I do eat fish, I don't eat any kind of meat. When I explained this to the woman who was managing the bar she said, "Salmon?" so I replied, "Si! Gracias." I was pleased that she was clearly offering me a tapa that was fish rather than meat.

I was sitting with my back to the bar, so John was the first to see what the waitress was bringing me along with his tapas: a huge piece of salmon, with lots of "patatas" (potatoes) and "ensalada" (salad). He could hardly hide his grin at the shock on my face when I was presented with a large plate instead of the expected tapa or slightly larger media ración (half portion).

When we went to pay the bill a young girl had appeared behind the bar. Judging by the proud expression on the manager's face when the girl said, "Ten euros please," in English, this was obviously her granddaughter. She looked even prouder when we congratulated her granddaughter on her good English.

While we were staying in Jumilla we went to a "Cata de vinos" (wine tasting) in one of the wine shops. The first wine expert spoke fluent English and gave us an English translation after speaking in Spanish, however at the same time she was showing a very professional PowerPoint presentation, which we managed to follow fairly easily. We told her not to worry about translating into English as we didn't want the locals to get too bored as they waited for the English explanations to finish.

The second wine expert only spoke in Spanish and his presentation seemed to go on forever. There were no slides to see and we only understood about 10% of what he was saying. We noticed that even the locals seemed to be getting restless, so I suspect that we weren't missing anything interesting. We weren't complaining though, as we had the chance to sample lots of good Jumilla wine. We also felt accepted by the local people, who were very welcoming and exchanged smiles and nods with us, so it was a very positive experience.

After a couple of days in town we realised that word must have got round about the British couple staying in one of the hotels. Every time we passed a group of young lads they would say, "Good morning" or "Good afternoon", and it was always with a smile.

One morning we had woken up early, so once we had finished our breakfast in the café next to the hotel, we decided to walk up the long, steep hill to the castillo (castle) overlooking the town, before it got too hot. On the way back down we agreed that, as it was still quite early in the day, we would have time before lunch to walk along a path near there that we had seen but never explored, and which looked interesting.

First though, we would have a coffee in Café Molowny, a restaurant we had noticed on the edge of Jumilla. There were quite a lot of cars parked outside and as soon as we entered the bar we could see that the place was packed with workmen having breakfast. The only available seats were a couple of stools, which meant sitting at the bar.

"I think we'll come back here for lunch," John said. We knew that Spanish workmen always went to the best, inexpensive restaurants, so the fact that they were all here having their breakfast was a good sign. It smelt delicious too!

After finishing our coffees we set off to find the path, which was signposted "Charco del Zorro". We followed the path, not sure exactly what we would find. We discovered that Charco del Zorro was a tranquil pool surrounded by wetlands, with good views of the Castillo, so the walk had proved worth doing.

"I've worked up a bit of an appetite," I said on the way back. "Your idea to go back to the restaurant for lunch sounds like a great plan, as it's the nearest place."

It was a good decision, as lunch was excellent. Although the waiter replied, "chicken" when we asked what was on the menu, once I explained that I didn't eat meat, he brought me a delicious bowl of seafood soup followed by a huge swordfish steak. I chose fruit for dessert as I was feeling quite full, however to my dismay I was presented with half a fresh pineapple, with all its leaves still on. John couldn't resist taking a photo of me staring in disbelief at my "light" dessert.

Tuesday is market day in Jumilla, so we decided to have a wander around. It looked like the whole town had the same idea, as the streets were packed with Jumillanos and their shopping trolleys.

Jumilla has a large indoor market, with mouth-watering displays of fresh fish and meat downstairs, and an array of fruit and vegetables upstairs. There were more fruit and vegetable stalls in the streets outside and all the produce looked remarkably fresh and appetising, probably because most of it had been grown locally. Murcia is renowned for its fine fruit and garden produce and for the intense flavour and vivid colours of the vegetables that are grown in the "huertas" (market gardens) on the outskirts of the city.

The streets near the indoor market had been closed to traffic, so we strolled around them looking at clothes, shoes, suitcases, household goods and the usual mix of market stalls, all at incredibly low prices. I was tempted by a brown lacy cardigan (well it was still quite early in the day, so my excuse was that it was a bit chilly). This only cost me five euros and it has been admired on more than one occasion since. I do love a bargain, so I suspected that the market would become a regular haunt once we moved there, and I have to admit to a couple more purchases, including some lovely red shoes.

On the outskirts of Jumilla, on the main road to Murcia that runs past the development at Santa Ana, we found out that there were a couple of large, well-stocked supermarkets. Even better, Mercadona (the Spanish equivalent of Sainsbury's) does home deliveries for a small fee.

"Once we are living here we won't have to walk back home laden with shopping," John said as he pointed the sign out to me. "If we do a big shop on Friday for the weekend we can get it delivered on Saturday morning."

We decided to walk from the edge of Jumilla to Residencial Santa Ana del Monte and time ourselves. It took us about forty-five minutes, so we agreed that we would probably rely on the Murcia bus unless we were feeling very energetic, however at least the walk home would be a possibility on a nice day if we managed to miss the bus.

The Surrounding Towns

We thought it would be a good idea to take the bus to Yecla on Wednesday, as that is their market day. We were obviously becoming biased already, as we thought the market there wasn't as good as the one in Jumilla. Yecla is bigger than Jumilla so there were plenty of streets for us to explore. It is an attractive town, with lots of historic buildings and a lovely plaza where we found the town hall, tourist office and the market.

On the way back to catch the Jumilla bus after roaming the streets of Yecla, we realised that it was time for lunch and were lucky enough to find a good restaurant close to the bus station. As soon as we opened the door to Meson María we knew it was a popular place by the level of noise inside. It was hardly surprising that it was so popular, as we had a good three course meal, with salad, bread, wine, water and coffee included, for 8.50 euros.

"Definitely one to remember for future visits," John commented as we left the restaurant.

Murcia was a bit further away and the bus there took just over an hour. Considering that it could take us almost that long to get into the centre of London from where we were living in south London, we reckoned that regular trips to Murcia would be quite feasible once we moved to Santa Ana. Having lived in London for so many years we imagine there will be times when we fancy the hustle and bustle of a city, so a cheap bus ride to Murcia will be on the cards. Murcia is a fascinating mixture of modern shops and historic sites, museums and art galleries with lots of restaurants for us to discover once we were living in the region.

We didn't spend all our time eating, drinking, shopping and taking the bus – we also did a fair bit of walking. It was well worth the climb up to Jumilla Castillo, as once we reached the top we had magnificent views of the whole town and we could just about make out our development at Santa Ana del Monte, in the distance. Another uphill walk that was very rewarding was the road up to the Monasterio de Santa Ana. Again the views were amazing, although this time we couldn't spot the development as it was hidden behind the trees on the other side of the mountain.

The woman in the local tourist office gave us a map of the town, which showed the historic tourist trail, as well as information on wine tours. At each point of interest in the town there is a plaque, which is in English as well as Spanish. We enjoyed walking around the streets of Jumilla following the trail and it was a good way to discover the many lovely historic buildings in the town.

We were particularly impressed with the Museo Arqueológico (Archaeological Museum), as not only were we given information in English at the front desk, but all around the museum there are signs in English. The Museo Jerónimo Molina (Municipal Museum) is also worth a visit and is one of my favourites, with its displays of household items from the past.

Jumilla boasts two national monuments: the magnificent 15th century church of Parroquia Mayor de Santiago and El Casón, a late Roman funeral edifice, dating back to the 5th century and the best of its kind still existing in Spain.

We also enjoyed visiting the Jardín Botánico (Botanical Gardens) just outside the town, even though it took us a while to find them as all we had to go on was an arrow on the edge of the tourist office map. I approached a young man who was sitting on a wall outside the Chapel of San Agustín and asked him which road led to the Jardín Botánico. He pointed to my map, indicating that there were two different ways of getting there, but unfortunately he did not tell us that one was the long, scenic route and the other one was a lot closer. We, of course, decided to take the road that turned out to be the long, scenic route. To be fair, he may not have realised that we didn't have a car and at least we managed to find the shorter route back into town again after we had enjoyed strolling round the gardens.

Needless to say, as keen wine drinkers, we also investigated some of the bodegas in the town. The Jumilla Denominación of Origin was created in 1966 and the main grape variety used is Monastrell. The climate, with its cold winters, mild springs and long, hot summers, and the lack of rain, make ideal conditions for these old vines, which produce deep, full-bodied wines. We were able to taste a selection of wines, from "vinos jovenes" (young, fresh wines) to powerful, intense "gran reservas" (wines aged for a minimum of five years), before choosing a couple of bottles to take home. Apart from the quality of the local wines, the prices are ridiculously cheap compared to what we would pay in the UK, especially when buying them at the bodegas rather than a supermarket or wine shop.

We also checked the local sporting facilities, as we knew that buying on a new development it might be a while before they completed all the facilities they were promising us. There is a large sports stadium on the edge of Jumilla with football pitches, tennis courts and several outdoor pools, plus indoor sports facilities within the town, including an indoor pool. We even discovered that there was an active athletics club, based at the sports stadium, although most of the members seemed to be juniors, with only a few male veteran runners and no female veterans.

"I hope that they are ready for a female veteran member," I said to John. "Once we move to Santa Ana I imagine we will want to join the athletics club."

"Supervet, you mean," was John's response. "Don't forget that you're over fifty now. I just hope that Jumilla is prepared for the sight of a señora of your advanced years running round the streets." He quickly moved out of reach before I could thump him.

You of course may have different priorities, so when you make your mind up about buying a new home, ensure that it meets all your requirements before signing on the dotted line.

John and I are fortunate enough to still be fit and healthy, however if you are thinking of retiring to Spain, and especially if you don't enjoy good health, a nearby medical centre plus proximity to a hospital will probably be top of your list. We know that the day may come when our health deteriorates, so we did make a note that there was a good health centre in Jumilla, and that there was a hospital nearby in Yecla. It would have been foolish not to have checked this out, even if it was low on our list of requirements. If you don't speak much Spanish you may also want to find out whether any doctors in the area speak English, especially if you are planning to live inland.

Don't forget the pharmacies for everyday ailments of course. After I had woken up one morning with a red eye I went into a pharmacy in Jumilla, having checked my Spanish phrase book for a couple of appropriate phrases, and I tried out my Spanish. The pharmacist looked at me, obviously realising that I was a foreigner and said, very slowly and carefully, "Do you speak English?" When I said that I did, and he realised that I was British, he then spoke rapidly in perfect English, questioning me on my symptoms and then prescribing some eye drops. We found out after we moved here that his mother is Irish, which explains why his English is so good.

Making Your Mind Up

Towards the end of our stay we phoned Mark and Stella to say that we had made our minds up. Jumilla has lots to offer: many interesting sights to see, good, reasonably priced restaurants and bars to visit, a weekly market plus several supermarkets, friendly locals, and the final important factor for John and me was that it is accessible by public transport for non-drivers. We felt that this was the right place for us to retire to in Spain and we were now ready to sign the contract for our new home at Residencial Santa Ana del Monte, Jumilla. Stella said that she would pick us up and drive us to the development, where we could decide which plot we wanted and pay the reservation fee.

The decision was made and we were both feeling very excited, but now unfortunately we had to get involved in what I consider to be "the boring bits". Paperwork, more paperwork and - being Spain - even more paperwork.

Sue Walker

CHAPTER SEVEN

The Boring Bits!

Finding our dream home in Spain was fun. It was just like being a child again in the sweet shop, clutching my pocket money and deciding what I would buy with my pennies. However after the excitement of finding somewhere that we both wanted to buy and which was within our budget, we came down to earth again and realised that there was a lot to be done before we would be able to sign on the dotted line.

In Spain, when you are buying "off plan" on a new development, you pay a nominal sum (3,000 euros in our case) to secure the plot you want. You then have a set period of time in which to check the contract, sign it and pay your deposit. The actual amount of deposit required varies but 30% seems to be the average. The balance, whether you are paying cash or getting a mortgage, will be required on completion.

The Legal Side

Unless you can afford to lose the money make sure that you have a Spanish lawyer to check the contract, preferably one who speaks good English unless your Spanish is particularly fluent. Whatever you do, don't use the same lawyer as the developer, and it is also advisable not to use a lawyer recommended by your agent, as there is a potential conflict of interest there.

Speak to any people you know who have already bought in Spain, research on the internet (you may get a recommendation through a forum), talk to people at property shows, but if possible try and get a personal recommendation.

One company that was recommended to us by an expert at a property show was the legalexgroup: *www.legalexgroup.com*, although by that time we already had our own solicitor, Sandra, who works for a Torrevieja company. She handles English-speaking clients and being able to deal with an English-speaking lawyer certainly made the legal process a lot easier for us. You should also ensure that you have a bank guarantee, before parting with any money. This is to cover you if the builder goes bust or if there are major problems and you need to claim your money back. It is important to check the contract to see what compensation clauses have been included, if any.

Stella picked us up at our hotel and then drove us first of all to the site at Santa Ana. There we spoke to Pablo in the sales office, who helped us pick the best position for our new house.

"It gets cold here in winter," he told us. "You want a south-facing property if you are going to be living here all year round. Apart from that it also depends on whether you want sun in the morning or in the evening."

John and I exchanged glances and he was the one who replied to Pablo, though I knew what he was going to say.

"We want the sun in the evening, so we can sit on our balcony with a glass of wine watching the sun go down." Pablo nodded in agreement, clearly appreciating our idea of the good life.

The next stop was in Torrevieja, at the developer San José's offices where contracts had been prepared, in English and in Spanish. As well as giving us the draft contract, they presented us with a bottle of wine – from Jumilla, where else?

Finally, our helpful chauffeuse Stella drove us to the solicitors' other office in Guardamar, where Sandra was based at that time.

Our Spanish lawyer Sandra speaks excellent English. She went through the contract very carefully, before telling us that there was something she was unhappy with and that she wanted the developer to provide us with a new contract. It was an incorrect date, which I thought we could have simply changed and initialled, but she was insistent that every detail had to be accurate before we signed anything. We wouldn't sign the contract until Sandra had received the replacement and said she was happy with it, which was very reassuring. As we were due to fly back to London Sandra told us that she would contact the developer and arrange for the corrected contract to be sent to our home address.

Sandra also gave us a quote for future costs, such as a mortgage to pay the balance due on completion and drawing up new Spanish wills, as our UK wills would not apply to our home in Spain. Spanish law does allow for UK citizens having UK wills, which you will still need for any assets in the UK; however you need to be aware of the difference in inheritance tax laws in Spain, which tend to favour children rather than spouses. As our plan was to become residents in Spain we knew it would be sensible to get Spanish wills too.

Sandra explained the various stages of buying a property in Spain to us, mentioning that at a future date we might want to sign a document in front of a notary, giving her power of attorney, so she could act on our behalf when we were in the UK.

The Padrón

"You already have your NIE numbers, so once you move over you should think of registering on the padrón," she suggested to us. "Every municipality in Spain has a record of local residents, which is known as the padrón. This is held at the "ayuntamiento" (town hall) and is similar to the electoral register in the UK."

Although it is not compulsory to be registered, it benefits both you and the municipality that you are living in. The level of funding that the local area receives depends on the number of people registered on the padrón, and as this funding is used for essential amenities such as the police and health centres, it is obvious why foreign residents should register so that basic services do not suffer because of insufficient funds.

Sandra explained that there are numerous advantages to having a "certificado de empadronamiento" (the certificate that is issued to you when you register on the padrón). If you have children it means you can enrol them in local schools – although our children of course are far too old for that! It also allows you to take advantage of any local leisure facilities with discounted rates at the municipal sports centre, which was of far greater interest to us. Sandra said we might also need it if we were looking for work locally.

Be Informed

On returning to London, realising how little we knew about the legal and financial aspects of buying abroad, I bought an excellent book called *Living in Spain* by Blevins Franks, although I have to say that if I read it too late in the day, it would send me to sleep. However, financial and legal matters do have that effect on some of us, so it is certainly no reflection on the authors.

Far more accessible to the layperson if you are buying in Murcia, is the excellent book by Debbie Jenkins: *Buying Property in Murcia.* Much of the advice is relevant even if you are thinking of buying a property in a different region, and there is plenty of good common sense, as well as stories about other ex-pats' experiences and the ingenious "Location-o-Meter", Debbie's tool for identifying the location to suit you. I only wish she had written it a bit earlier, as it would have helped us understand the buying process a lot better and would have helped us avoid the pitfalls lying ahead of us!

I have already emphasised the importance of having an independent lawyer and this had proved the point. You should act with the same caution that you would use if buying a property in the UK, but in addition you must be aware that there are differences between the two countries and not assume that your contract will protect you in the same way as a contract drawn up back home. We were to discover the significance of this at a later date.

While we were at the developer's office we had paid the reservation fee and had been given a receipt for this payment. This meant that there would be time for Sandra to ensure the contract was correct before it was sent to our London home, and time for us to sign and return it, as well as making arrangements to transfer the rest of our deposit.

Currency Exchange

Although we were both rather naive when it came to buying property abroad, one thing we had learnt from our many visits to property shows was that it makes sense to use a currency exchange company rather than your own bank when transferring money to Spain, especially when large sums were involved. There are many currency exchange companies around who will give you a better rate than the high streets banks, plus they will ensure that you don't have to pay receiving charges, which are commonly charged by Spanish banks. You can register with several companies for no cost, then shop around for the best deal when you are ready to transfer funds.

An alternative is to pay the company a 10% deposit and ask them to wait for an agreed exchange rate for you, which is known as forward buying. This is useful if the current exchange rate is quite low and you have time to wait for an improvement in the rate, although you also run the risk of the rate dropping even lower.

Some companies set a minimum amount for the funds you are transferring if it is a one-off payment, and will charge a fee if you transfer less than that. They also have the facility to transfer funds for you on a regular basis, which is particularly useful if, like us, you are going to be retiring to Spain and will be transferring your pension to a Spanish account either monthly or quarterly. They will usually guarantee the exchange rate for one or two years, so you have to decide whether you want to agree a rate for that period of time. You risk losing out if the pound gets stronger, but at least you don't have to worry about the pound weakening, plus you have the advantage of knowing how much money you will be receiving each month.

We also needed to get a Spanish bank account, even though we wouldn't be living there for a couple of years. Stella helped us with this, recommending that we open an account in the nearest town to our new home, which was Jumilla. As we were staying in Jumilla at the time it made sense to organise this whilst we were there. Although we have been told that everything that you do in Spain involves a lot of paperwork, this particular process seemed simpler than it is in the UK, and with a bit of help from Stella, both in ensuring that we had the right documents and in translating for us, we were soon the proud owners of a bank pass book for the CAM bank in Jumilla.

As soon as we returned to the UK, we contacted Global Currency Exchange *www.gcen.co.uk/* to find out what rate they were offering, which seemed very competitive, so we transferred the money to them ready for when we had signed the contract. We chose this particular company because friends recommended it, and certainly we were impressed by their efficiency as much as their rates. Since then, we have used other companies and found them equally efficient, so it is a case of shopping around whenever you need to transfer your money abroad.

The contract arrived not long after we had returned home, so we signed and returned it, transferred our money via the currency exchange company and only then did we realise the enormity of what we had just done.

"We are soon going to be the owners of a new home in Spain," John looked just as excited as I felt. "In just over eighteen months' time we will be able to take our holidays at Santa Ana and the following year we will be able to retire there."

"I think this calls for a celebration," was my response. "It's time to crack open that bottle of cava that we brought back home!"

We were definitely naive, as we eventually found out. We loved Spain for its relaxed way of life, however over the next few years we would discover that this attitude also had a downside. People may joke about the "mañana, mañana" attitude in Spain (everything is going to happen "tomorrow" - and as we know tomorrow never comes) – but we were impatient to be staying in our dream home, and although we were prepared to have a wait, which is inevitable when you buy an off-plan property, we didn't realise quite how long that wait would be.

However at that time it seemed that life was good, our future was also looking very bright and we went to bed happy. But just when you think life is treating you well, it has a habit of kicking you in the teeth. We were living in a dream world, and I, for one, was soon going to have to wake up and face up to the real world.

Sue Walker

CHAPTER EIGHT

My Annus Horribilis

The year had begun with great promise and excitement as we had at long last found our dream home. Over the following months we told all our friends and families about our decision and they shared our excitement - no doubt that was partly because of the thought of future holidays in the sun.

The only worry on the horizon was my mother's health. When I had decided to work part-time one reason was the opportunity to build up my business as a complementary therapist, however I was also all too aware that my mother was in her eighties and the time might come when she wasn't as fit and healthy as she had been. Not that I would have dared say that to her! She was proud of the fact that she was still playing badminton in her eighties, plus tennis in the summer months and going on long walks with her younger friends.

Mum lived in the northeast of England and I was living in London, so I didn't get to see her as often as I would have liked. Fortunately her younger sister and brother-in-law lived nearby, so they visited her on a regular basis. My uncle phoned me during the summer to say that they were concerned about my mother, who was becoming very confused at times, and that somebody would need to keep an eye on her when they went on holiday in two weeks' time.

"Thanks for the notice," I thought to myself, but I appreciated all that my uncle and aunt were doing for my mother, so all I said to them was that I would book my train to Newcastle and stay with her while they were away.

To be honest, I thought Mum seemed fine while I was staying with her, though maybe a little bit frail. She had enjoyed good health all her life, in spite of enjoying her glass of gin in the evening and the occasional cigarette. My mother was called Joy and I always felt that she more than lived up to her name. She looked at the photos that I had taken at Santa Ana del Monte and I knew that she was pleased to see how happy I was when I told her about my future new home in Spain.

"You can fly to Alicante from Newcastle," I told her. "You will be able to have lots of cheap holidays with us in Spain!"

I decided to go and visit my mother later that year so that I could spend her birthday with her and booked the train as soon as I got back to London. Shortly before I was due to travel up north again I had another phone call from my uncle, telling me that my mother had collapsed and been taken to hospital. It was a tremendous shock, as my mother was never ill, so when I caught the train to Newcastle I was very concerned. The news wasn't good: my mother had cancer and it was too advanced for the doctors to be able to give us much hope. She was discharged from hospital but not well enough to go home, so they decided to move her to a care home.

Over the next few months the train journey to Newcastle became a regular event. My three children travelled north with me just after Christmas, hoping that they could take their Gran to a hotel near the care home for a Christmas meal, but sadly by the time we arrived she was back in hospital again. Mum was delighted to have so many of the family there and seemed to be her usual lively self, so it was a happy occasion for all of us.

At the end of January I had the phone call that I had been dreading: my mother had died in her sleep. It wasn't unexpected and I had to be grateful that she hadn't suffered for long, but it was still a painful time for me.

Things Get Worse

Worse was to come. Two months later, while I was out having a couple of drinks with friends, my uncle rang me on my mobile, saying that he had tried my home number but there was no reply. I couldn't quite hear him with the background noise in the pub, so I went outside into the street.

"Sue, I'm sorry pet, but I have some very bad news for you," my uncle said. My immediate reaction was that something must have happened to my aunt, so I couldn't really comprehend what he said next. "Stephen has died."

"What?" This had to be a bad dream. "Not Steve…!" He was my youngest brother, nearly ten years' younger than me. I still had vivid memories of him as a baby, splashing happily in the bath, and as a young child, insisting on playing tennis with an adult racket that was nearly as big as him.

"He died last night in his sleep but nobody knows any more than that. Florence phoned me this morning and I said that I would let you know."

It couldn't be true. My brother Steve, who was only forty-nine, couldn't be dead. I stood there in the street, tears streaming down my face, until John realised that something must be wrong and came out to find me.

I only have a vague recollection of John putting his arms round me, listening to what I was mumbling and then taking me home. Once I was back in the house I had to phone my children and break the news to them, then ring my other brother David.

Unlike me, Steve loved golf. I had told him that we were going to be living on a golf development and he had been looking forward to visiting us for a golfing holiday. Life can be cruel and it can also be ironic. After the funeral we went to Steve's local golf club for the wake, where we spoke to his golfing friends as well as his many other friends and family. The whole family was devastated by this second funeral, but life had to go on and we all had many happy memories of Mum and Steve to treasure.

To be quite honest, I found it hard to cope over the following months, but John and my three children helped me through this difficult period of my life. My work colleagues were also very understanding and supportive; however I lost a lot of my enthusiasm for my part-time job at the College and even for my work as a complementary therapist.

Birthday Celebrations

I needed something to make me think more positively, and my family too needed to have a happy occasion to look forward to, so I decided that I would have a huge party to celebrate my sixtieth birthday, inviting all my family and friends. Not only that, I would plan a holiday to – where else? – Spain. After all, I would now officially be a pensioner (or "pensionista" in Spanish), even though I wasn't quite ready to retire yet.

It was a fabulous party: the sun shone on us and it was lovely to see so many old friends as well as my three children, John's family, my brother David and many other family members. My daughter Kate had organised a delicious birthday cake, which thankfully didn't have sixty candles on it or I would never have managed to blow them all out!

The following day we travelled first class on Eurostar to Paris, where we caught the Trenhotel to Barcelona.

We paid just over £100 each for our private two-bed "Gran Clase" sleeper, which had its own toilet and shower. Dinner with wine and breakfast were included in the price, which we thought was a reasonable deal.

Having spent the day walking around Paris, the first thing we wanted to do on boarding our train was to have a lovely warm shower. We hadn't even had time to get dressed again before there was a knock outside, so John opened the door with a towel wrapped around him. We were being advised by the steward to go to the restaurant carriage as soon as possible if we wanted to be sure of getting a table, otherwise we might have to eat a lot later. John was amazed to see how quickly I could get ready when I was hungry and didn't want to wait for dinner!

We assumed that there would be two sittings and that we might be asked to move once we had finished our meal, however that was not the case. The menu gave us a wide choice, with meat for John, plenty of fish dishes for me and also some vegetarian choices. The wine list was also extensive, and we were able to choose whatever wine we wanted. We enjoyed a delicious dinner, which was a lot tastier than airline food, with plenty of wine flowing and time to relax and enjoy the experience. We finished with coffee and liqueurs before returning to our cabin, to find that the beds had already been made up ready for us to fall into them.

If you are going to take the Trenhotel we would advise using the earplugs that you will find in the toiletries bag they provide you with, especially if you are a light sleeper. John did not sleep too well as the train rattled its way noisily through the French countryside, although my sleep wasn't disturbed too much.

We woke up to find that we had crossed into Spain and, as our train continued south, we went to the dining car for breakfast. After enjoying the continental breakfast, we returned to our cabin to find that our beds had been tidied away, so we could sit in comfort until the train drew into Barcelona station.

For the latest prices and further details on the Trenhotel, if you want to travel by train from Paris to either Barcelona or Madrid, look at *www.seat61.com/Spain.htm*. We definitely enjoyed the experience and would recommend that you try it at least once. Our next stop was Tarragona, a city that we had never visited before, which proved to be a fascinating historic place, with many well-preserved Roman monuments. One of the most notable landmarks is the Roman Amphitheatre, which overlooks the sea. As John said; "If you like looking at old ruins, it is definitely worth a visit. Some of us take old ruins with us, of course!" Sometimes he pushes his luck.

We then stayed in Salou for a couple of nights. On arrival in Salou we visited the tourist office where we picked up a leaflet that gave details of a mediaeval procession that was taking place the following evening.

According to the leaflet the show was due to start at 8pm, so we headed towards the castle just after eight, expecting to see the procession already coming towards us. The streets had been closed off and policemen were standing there, but all the participants seemed to be hanging around chatting and smoking, with no signs of the parade starting.

When the procession eventually set off, it was very impressive and worth waiting to see. Damsels swirled around, holding hands, as they danced along the streets, drummers marched along as they beat their drums and there were even jugglers tossing flaming torches into the air and somehow managing to catch them. Once the procession had passed us, we slipped through the back streets to find the restaurant where we had gone earlier to reserve a table for dinner. It was lucky that we had booked as it became very busy, with many of the participants, still in their costumes, coming in for something to eat, as well as lots of the spectators.

I have to say that Salou wasn't our idea of Spain, and it wasn't somewhere we would want to return to, as there were far too many British and German bars and restaurants there. We went to Cambrils for the day and the charming traditional Spanish fishing village was more to our liking, especially when we found a lovely Spanish restaurant where we had the "menú del día" (menu of the day). We paid ten euros each for three courses, a basket of bread and some drinks: a real bargain, especially as it was a Sunday and many places only offer a menú del día during the week.

The final leg of our journey took us to Alicante, from where we had decided to catch the bus to Jumilla. We knew what time it left the bus station, but unfortunately we hadn't been able to find out how long the journey would take. Not only did it take us over an hour, but the bus suddenly stopped in the middle of Novelda and we were told to get off.

"What's going on?" I asked John, but he was as puzzled as I was, because this hadn't been mentioned when we bought our tickets.

"I can see another bus ahead of us," he said. "Maybe we have to transfer to that one." Sure enough, we had to board the second bus, which eventually took us to Jumilla. We reached our hotel a lot later than anticipated and were very relieved to discover that the restaurant next door was open for dinner.

Why No Progress?

The few days that we spent in Jumilla seemed to fly by, as we were still discovering more about the town. We were keen to visit the site at Santa Ana to find out how the building was progressing, but it proved to be a bit of a concern.

"They don't seem to have done much since our last visit," was John's immediate reaction. "I think more foundations have been completed and there are lots of bricks lying around, but I would have expected them to be actually building up by now."

"I think we should contact Mark and Stella when we get back home," I replied. "Maybe they can get an update for us."

It had been a fantastic holiday, but we flew back to London with lots of questions that needed answering. Our property wasn't due to be completed until the following spring, but we knew that many people had expected to be living there by now. Whatever was happening at Santa Ana del Monte?

Sue Walker

CHAPTER NINE

A Funny Thing Happened On The Way To The Forum

Over the next few months we were in constant contact with Stella and Mark by email, as we expressed our concerns and they reassured us that delays were common when buying off-plan. No doubt their hearts sank when they saw yet another email from me in their inbox.

Working part-time meant that I had plenty of free time to surf the net at home when John was at work, and through Google I discovered there were a lot of helpful websites for ex-pats in Spain, including one dedicated to buyers at Sante Ana del Monte. We joined the off-plan developments forum on a couple of these websites and this opened our eyes to the potential problems when buying a new property in Spain.

We made friends with other buyers on-line, shared all our worries with them, and even met many of them during a weekend in Torquay, at a hotel owned by a couple of our potential new neighbours. I hasten to add that they were not called Sybil and Basil, and were very attentive hosts. Many of our fellow buyers expressed their concerns about the delays at Santa Ana and we agreed that we could keep each other updated whenever any of us visited the site.

At the beginning of 2008 it was officially announced that there was a delay to the development and our new home, which should have been ready in January 2008, still only had its foundations. Stella told us that our new completion date was now December 2008.

I had made the decision to retire earlier than planned and handed in my notice at the College. My colleagues joked that they were not happy at this decision, saying that I had promised to work there until the following year, but then brightened up at the thought of coming to visit me in Spain.

Not long after I had resigned John also made a momentous decision.

"I have decided to go for early retirement too," he announced, and was rewarded with a big hug and a kiss from me. "I think we will both feel a lot happier if we are living out there and can keep an eye on the development."

We had a couple of options: we knew some people were living in apartments on the coast owned by San José, the company that was building our new home, and we could see if any more were available; another was to rent a townhouse at Playa Golf, also on the coast, which was another development built by San José. The final option was to see if there were any properties to rent in Jumilla.

Moving To Spain

We flew to Alicante shortly after I had finished working: to celebrate my retirement and also to start the search for somewhere to live until the end of the year. We were renting a house at Playa Golf for four days and then spending a couple of nights in Jumilla.

The owner of the property had left us strict instructions, which we had to follow every time we left the house, even during the day time. All the shutters had to be closed and then fastened with a large metal clip, the alarm had to be put on, the front door secured with a double lock and even the gate had to be locked behind us. Even more bizarre, we were given orders not to put any toilet paper down the toilet!

We met up with Rachel, who would be living near us at Santa Ana del Monte once all our houses had been completed, and she showed us around the apartment that San José had provided for her. It was fine but rather noisy as it was far too close to the main road, so we eliminated that option.

By the second day of our visit John announced that he had had enough of staying at Playa Golf.

"We're going to head for Jumilla," he informed me, in a tone that meant I shouldn't argue with him. Not that I intended doing so, as I'd been thinking of suggesting it myself. "There's no way I would want to live here – I've already seen all that I want to see – and the sooner we look for somewhere to rent in Jumilla the better."

"That's the best idea you've had for a long time," I replied. "We'll contact the hotel and say we'd like to check in a couple of days earlier than planned and then see if Stella is able to take us to the bus station in Torrevieja."

Renting An Apartment

Because we had both been working we hadn't done the really sensible thing and rented for a while before looking for a property to buy, however now that we had both decided to take early retirement we realised that there was no reason to wait for our new home to be ready. We could rent an apartment until we were able to move into our house in Santa Ana and Jumilla was the obvious place to rent somewhere as it was only a few miles away from the development. We didn't want to waste any more time.

When our bus arrived in Jumilla we were both excited at the prospect of living there for the nine months until our house was ready to move into. We agreed that we would start our search for somewhere to rent first thing in the morning.

We spent a rainy day walking the streets of Jumilla and visiting all the estate agents to see if they had any property to rent. We looked at a large old apartment, overlooking the main street. It was a good central location, though we did wonder how noisy it would be living there when the landlady proudly told us we could watch the processions and hear the music from the balcony. Apart from concerns about the noise levels, we decided that it was a bit too big for us anyway.

Another property that we viewed was a modern apartment, overlooking the park. The young man from the estate agent's office really loved it and sat down on the modern leather sofa as he extolled the virtues of the apartment. We had noticed though that it was on the first floor and there was a bar on the corner of the block. Knowing how the Spanish love to sit outside on a summer's evening with a "cerveza" (beer) or glass of wine, chatting loudly with their friends, we agreed that this wasn't the place for us. We also felt that it was too modern and somehow lacked character. So we told him "no" and left him sitting there, shaking his head sadly and clearly of the opinion that the British couple were mad not to take it.

The last property that we saw was also an old traditional Spanish apartment, although not quite as big as the first one. It had a spacious living room, a balcony overlooking the town with good views of the mountains, a reasonably sized kitchen, a bathroom, additional separate toilet and three large bedrooms. The man from the rental agency, Habitacasa, knew that we were looking at other properties, so we promised to go back on Friday morning and let him know our decision.

On our final day in Jumilla we returned to Habitacasa and told the agent, Manuel, that we wanted to rent the apartment from the beginning of April. His English was even more limited than our Spanish, so we rang Stella and then handed him the phone. She explained to him what we wanted to do and found out from him that we would have to pay 150 euros as a sign of our intent to rent the apartment. The remainder of the rental deposit would be paid when we signed the contract, as well as the first month's rent.

Manuel carefully wrote out a receipt, showing us his identity card so that we could check the number was written down correctly and copying John's NIE number painstakingly, while I glanced at my watch and wondered if we would be in time to catch the bus to Murcia. Surely twenty minutes is more than enough time to write out a receipt? Obviously it's not, when you are in Spain.

Luckily the bus was a bit late, so we managed to catch it. We had already noticed that whenever you buy tickets at the local bus station the time the bus is due is printed on them followed by "approx". This means that buses are rarely late: if the 10.00 "approx" bus doesn't get there until 10.10, you can't really complain that it should have been there at 10.00, can you? I like the Spanish logic. In future I will tell John I am meeting him at a particular time "approx"- that should stop him complaining about my punctuality!

The rental contract was sent to our solicitor in Guardamar, who checked it carefully and told us it would be fine to sign the agreement. At the beginning of April we returned to Jumilla to take over the apartment. Stella had agreed to meet us and help with any translations that were required as, although our Spanish was gradually improving, it was not good enough to cope with legal and property matters.

We went back to Habitacasa, where Manuel sat us all down and then slowly read out each clause on the rental contract, whilst Stella helped us with anything that we couldn't understand. The landlord and his wife were going to meet us at the apartment, where everybody would sign the contract and we would hand over the money in return for our keys. When we got to the apartment we all had to sit down again while Manuel slowly read out each clause on the contract, this time for the landlords' benefit.

Once this was done the four of us had to sign each page of the three copies of the contract (one for us, one for the landlords and one for Manuel). As the landlord's signature was just a squiggle, he had to print his ID number underneath each time he signed a page, and John had to write his NIE number underneath as his signature was just as bad. Luckily the two women present had legible signatures, so we didn't take quite as long signing the pages.

We had arranged to meet at Manuel's office at 10.30, as we planned to take Stella out for lunch before she had to drive back to her office on the coast. By the time contracts were signed and money and keys exchanged I was starting to feel hungry, however we still weren't ready to leave. Our landlord took us round the apartment, showing us how to turn on the gas, light the oven, use the washing machine etc. We also had to carefully check that everything listed in "Anexo Uno" (Annex One) was present and correct, before we all signed it.

At long last we thanked them and walked towards the front door, thinking we could now head to the restaurant, but we were not quite finished. The lady who lived in the apartment opposite ours came out of her door as we were about to go into the lift and she had to be introduced to everyone. Another long conversation ensued, with lots of smiles and nods, until we finally shook everybody's hand and left to go to Casa Sebastian, the restaurant we had selected for lunch.

I glanced at my watch: it was already well after 1.30, which was hardly a surprise as my stomach had been feeling hollow for nearly an hour. We had a lovely lunch with Stella, thanked her again for all her help, and went back to our new home in Jumilla. That evening we celebrated by sitting on our balcony, enjoying a glass of cava, as we watched the sun setting over the mountains.

"Well, you've got your balcony and your mountain view earlier than we expected," I said to John as we clinked our glasses.

"Hopefully by the end of the year we will be in our own house and with our own balcony," he replied. "Though I'm not sure we will want to be sitting outside at the end of December!"

We were both feeling very positive and the future was looking a lot brighter. We now had a flat where we could stay in the middle of Jumilla and our new life in Spain had begun. Our next visit would be for a holiday in May and we were planning to move over permanently in June.

As soon as we returned to London we would tell all our new friends on the forum about our exciting news. Many of them planned to visit Santa Ana over the next few months to check how their new homes were progressing, but we would be able to give them regular updates. We still expected to be moving into our own new home by the date the developer had promised us, however before then we could watch the development grow and see our house being built. Yes, we were definitely naive.

Sue Walker

CHAPTER TEN

The Nightmare Begins...
Is Our Dream Over?

I was considering calling this chapter "The Rain in Spain Falls Everywhere!" We returned to Spain for our holiday in May and it started raining after our first few days in Denia. We spent most of a day trip to Calpe sheltering in restaurants and bars and we then went by train to Alicante, where it poured down while we were staying there too, before heading to our apartment in Jumilla. Guess what? It rained on our first day in Jumilla, but after that the weather improved and for the rest of our stay it was lovely and sunny.

I'm not saying that I am superstitious, but on 13th May I received a text from Heather, one of my friends from the forum.

"Sue, are you aware of the news about San José - I think you're away at the moment? They've gone into voluntary liquidation. Log on to the forum if you can. Text me if you need to. Heather."

I couldn't say anything as I was so shaken by this news, so I just handed my mobile to John to let him read the message too.

"Come on, we need to get to an internet café and find out more," John said. "We don't know what the implications are, but hopefully we can get more details through the forum."

My legs were actually shaking when we walked up the street to the nearest internet café. This wasn't happening, it was just a bad dream and I would wake up in a minute. We had been assured by our agent, and also by our solicitor, that licences were in place, the company was stable and that there shouldn't be any problems with our purchase.

The news was true and it wasn't looking good, but we spoke to Stella, our agent, who said she was trying to find out more about the situation and would get back to us as soon as she could.

Voluntary Liquidation

"Try not to worry," Stella said. It was too late for that, as we were both extremely anxious, however there was nothing we could do as we were due to fly back to the UK.

True to her word Stella rang us back the following day and informed us that the company had gone into voluntary liquidation to protect themselves while they tried to raise the finance for the final building licences.

"Once they have the money they will be able to continue building at Santa Ana del Monte. It shouldn't delay the development by too much," Stella tried to reassure us. We felt a little bit better, as she seemed to be so optimistic, but deep down we weren't entirely convinced by her words.

Once back in the UK we didn't have time to sit around worrying as we had a house to get ready to sell, lots of clearing out to do (mainly me, of course), several farewell parties to organise and we were due to move to Spain in less than four weeks' time. Needless to say, the next few weeks flew by. We had packed two large suitcases each, as we had decided to go by train again, though on this occasion we had booked the Trenhotel from Paris to Madrid.

Although I was excited at the thought that my dream was beginning to come true and looking forward to making a permanent move to Spain, I was inevitably feeling a bit sad at leaving my children behind in London. We had a lovely family meal at the Criterion restaurant and I told them that it wouldn't be that long until we saw them again as we planned to come over a couple of times before the flat was sold. After all, I still had most of my winter clothes to take over to Spain, as I had been told that it can get pretty cold in winter when you are living inland.

Saying Goodbye

I had made all of my farewells, my packed cases were bulging and all we had to do was head to St Pancras International station to catch the Eurostar train to Paris. John as usual insisted that we left in plenty of time, so when we arrived at St Pancras we were far too early for our train.

I was about to suggest that we treat ourselves to a drink in the Champagne Bar, but John beat me to it.

"Why don't we go and try out the Champagne Bar? We have more than enough time to have a drink there."

As we approached the bar I spotted two familiar figures perched on bar stools and didn't know whether to laugh or to cry as my daughters came over and hugged me.

"I assume that you knew about this?" I turned to John, who gave me a guilty smile. "Yes, but I promised them I wouldn't tell you."

"Mark is on his way," Kate told me. "We have all taken a day's leave to see you off. Now, I assume that you would like champagne?"

"You don't need to ask Mum," Vicky said before I could reply. My daughter knows me only too well.

It was a fantastic send-off and as the train pulled out of the station I felt a sense of anticipation. Our new adventure had begun in style and we were about to embark on an exciting journey. For the moment, I put all my worries about Santa Ana del Monte behind me. I wanted to make the most of the next few days.

Although we didn't have much time in Paris I didn't mind too much, as it is a city that we have visited many times before and after all we were heading for Madrid, the capital city of our soon-to-be new country. Again we had a superb dinner on the train and we slept slightly better as this time we knew to use the earplugs, eventually waking up just outside Madrid. We had decided to stay a few nights there before continuing our journey to Murcia.

Madrid

We already knew that the custom in many Spanish restaurants is to offer you a glass of brandy or liqueur on the house when they bring you coffee at the end of your evening meal. We were surprised however when this happened in Madrid, as we cannot imagine any London restaurant bringing a free drink with the bill, no matter how much you had paid for your meal.

On our first night in Madrid a bottle of cherry brandy was left on the table at the end of our meal, so in theory we could have helped ourselves to several glasses, though in practice one small glass was more than enough for us. In another restaurant our waitress brought over several different bottles of liqueurs so we could choose which one we wanted to try.

The most surprising episode though was after we had lunch in a small restaurant in the centre of Madrid. I popped into the ladies toilet on the way out and emerged to find that John had already paid the bill and was waiting in the street outside. In spite of this, our waitress stopped me and insisted that we were to have a drink on the house, so I had to haul John back inside while the waitress poured two substantial glasses of brandy for us.

"This is fine while we are on holiday, however I think that now we are going to be living in Spain permanently we will have to limit how often we eat out. Either that or we will have to go on regular detoxes!" I said to John.

"Don't worry, remember that you're a pensioner," he teased me. "You won't be able to afford to have meals out as often now."

In Spain, every meal in a restaurant should come with a health warning that it may include large quantities of alcohol.

We had gone to a restaurant near our hotel on our final evening, thinking that we would probably have a meal there later on, but that we would have a drink first and maybe a tapa so that we could check when they started serving dinner. The waiter apologised and said that they wouldn't be open for dinner, but suggested a couple of other places that we could try. When he brought over our drinks the waiter also brought us some potato skins topped with melting cheese, which proved to be very filling and delicious tapas and which didn't appear on our bill.

Our strangest experience was when we went out for breakfast near our hotel in Madrid. Breakfast wasn't included and we thought that the hotel's offering was a bit pricey at eleven euros each, so we had decided to investigate the local cafés. There was one in the shopping centre near the hotel, which had the widest selection of breakfasts that we have ever stumbled across, including Scottish, Irish and Spanish variations. The set breakfasts included drinks, which were mainly coffee or tea, however we noticed that there was a choice of beer or wine with the Spanish option. We knew we were being a bit decadent, but on our last morning staying in Madrid we decided that we just had to try a beer and a glass of wine. It would have been rude not to.

We had started our trip in style and wanted to finish it in style too, so we travelled "preferente" (first class) from Madrid to Murcia. As well as having very comfortable seats, you are served a first class meal with drinks, though you have to order vegetarian meals at least twenty-four hours in advance. We really enjoyed the journey as the countryside we passed through was lovely, and although it took nearly four hours, it didn't seem that long. The food and drinks of course helped to pass the time, as dining in Spain, whether on a train or in a restaurant, is always a leisurely occasion. We could have also watched a video as we were provided with headphones and a film was being shown on the screens in our carriage.

When we eventually arrived at our new home in Jumilla I still felt a sense of anticipation. Although the journey was now over, we had an exciting new life to look forward to. We weren't sure what the future held and there were still major concerns regarding Santa Ana, but whatever happened we knew we wouldn't have any regrets.

"This calls for a celebration." John had poured a couple of glasses of red Jumilla wine. "To our new life in Spain!"

"Whatever it may bring," I replied. "Cheers! Things can only get better."

Looking back, perhaps the Labour slogan wasn't the best one to choose. However as we sat outside on our balcony, gazing towards the mountains surrounding Jumilla, we knew that we had no regrets about our decision to move here and we were both excited about our future life in Spain.

CHAPTER ELEVEN

¿Habla Inglés?

This wasn't a question we wanted to ask as we were now living in a Spanish town, so why should we expect the local people to speak English? However over the next couple of months there were several occasions when we wished that either we spoke more Spanish or the person we were dealing with spoke at least some English.

We had invested in a large Spanish dictionary, which we didn't want to carry around with us all the time, but our pocket dictionary wasn't much good when discussing delays in getting my USB modem and it was even less helpful when I couldn't get access to the internet and was trying to find out why.

As we were renting our flat we couldn't make any alterations to it, so we decided that getting broadband installed would have to wait until we had our own house. Mobile broadband seemed the ideal solution, as we wanted to have internet access to keep in touch with friends and family, and so I decided to venture into our local Vodafone shop.

Getting Internet Access

I had my passport, NIE number and bank book, knowing that in Spain you usually need as much paperwork as possible before trying to carry out any kind of transaction. The staff seemed unsure whether I had the right papers, but after half an hour they managed to print off a form in triplicate for me to sign. I stood there expectantly, imagining in my innocence that I would be handed the modem and could go straight home to check my emails. The shop assistant gave me a quizzical look and, when I managed to convey the message that I was waiting for my modem, she shrugged her shoulders. I had to come back next week, she told me.

"Lunes?" I suggested, as it was Tuesday and I assumed it would only take a couple of days for the USB modem to arrive, so next Monday would be fine.

She looked amazed at the idea of it being there by Monday. "No. Miércoles…" she replied, with a note of doubt in her voice that suggested she wasn't entirely convinced it would arrive by then. When I went back into the shop the following Wednesday I wasn't too surprised when once again I was told to return next week.

Two weeks later and my modem had arrived, and I was greeted with big smiles from all the staff, who were clearly happy that their customer was going to be satisfied, although unfortunately my friend in the Vodafone shop was unable to print off the guarantee. She pointed to her printer, which apparently wasn't working, and again said to come back next week.

Eventually I had my modem, which I am happy to say was working satisfactorily, plus my guarantee had successfully been printed, so all was well between me and Vodafone. At least all was well for the next two months, until one day in September when I had an error message, saying "a connection to the remote computer could not be established", so once again I went to visit my friends in the Vodafone shop, who seemed pleased to see me in spite of all the extra work I was giving them. I told them what the error message had said and they informed me it was a problem with coverage. When would it be fixed? "Next week maybe?" I asked optimistically. This time they had no idea, and at the time of writing (three months' later), I still can't use my lovely modem, although to be fair to Vodafone, they aren't charging me anything. Thankfully, John has a WIFI enabled laptop so I am able to keep in touch with everybody on this.

"I can't use my laptop anymore as Sue is always using it," John keeps complaining. Do I complain when he wants to watch football on TV? Of course not. As far as I am concerned I have no case to answer.

Meeting New Friends

In July we discovered that the Ruta del Vino Jumilla (Jumilla Wine Route) was organising a series of events in the bodegas: "Música entre Vinos", which sounded a good combination to us, as music-lovers who have been known to enjoy the occasional glass of wine. After the second event we stood talking to several of the young musicians, who spoke a bit of English, when a señora approached us to ask if we were English and where we came from. She told us she was called Juana María and she seemed delighted when we told her that we were originally from London but now lived in Jumilla.

Juana María teaches English privately and was keen to improve her pronunciation, so she suggested that we could meet up every week for a coffee, to give us an opportunity to learn more Spanish and for her to practise her English. We now see her twice a week for café y tostadas (coffee and toasted baguettes), to talk in both English and Spanish and above all to have a good laugh together.

As well as Juana María, we have met many members of her family: during the recent "Semana Gastronómica" (Gastronomic Week) in Jumilla, a group of us went for Sunday lunch to Hotel Casa Luzón, where we enjoyed a superb meal as well as excellent wine from Jumilla - where else?

We have met other ex-pats living in the area, but we would highly recommend trying to get to know the local people if you want to become part of the community. We are fortunate in knowing Juana María, who speaks very good English. Through her we can find out what is going on in Jumilla and it also helps us to understand more about Spanish culture and traditions.

The Language

Our Spanish is slowly improving and we can now manage to go shopping, dine out, catch the local bus to Murcia, and carry out other daily activities without needing to refer to the dictionary.

Spanish children start learning English at quite a young age. We were having a drink and some tapas in one of our favourite haunts, Bar Paraiso, when we heard some children at the table behind us practising their English, possibly because they had heard us talking to each other. We turned round and spoke to them and they were soon happily trying out their English on us. "Bye bye!" they all chorused when we eventually left the bar.

On another occasion, we were sitting in Bar Duque de Lerma when we heard the daughter of the señora who works there chanting: "Amarillo - yellow. Azul - blue." Not bad, considering that she is only four years' old.

One of our local supermarkets is Consum and the staff there all know us and say "hola" when they see us, even when we are walking along the street. One day when I was paying for my shopping with a couple of twenty-euro notes, I realised that the cashier was scrutinising them carefully, holding them up to the light. I must have looked worried, because she said something in Spanish which I couldn't quite catch and then repeated in perfect English, "There have been some fake notes, but don't worry, these are OK." Previously she had only spoken in Spanish to us, so I was surprised at how good her English was.

Should We Stay Or Should We Go?

August was approaching and this meant that most of Spain would be closing down for the summer holidays, including the Mercantile Court in Alicante, who were dealing with the administration process. John and I realised that serious decisions would have to be made about our dream property. We were receiving conflicting information on the owners' forum: some people were forecasting gloom and doom, prophesising that San José and, more importantly, Herrada del Tollo (the subsidiary company responsible for building at Santa Ana del Monte) were on the verge of bankruptcy; others were confident that San José would obtain the necessary finance and that everybody would have their house. Even the optimists though were saying that the first houses wouldn't be ready for at least another eighteen months.

"Can we afford to wait until then?" I asked John. "Should we abandon our dream and return to the UK?"

"No," John didn't hesitate. "I don't think we can afford to wait for Santa Ana del Monte to be completed, but why would you want to go back to London? We've got better weather in Spain, the cost of living is less, the wine is excellent and cheap, and we have already made some good friends here. Our friends and family back in the UK will be more than happy to visit us in Jumilla and probably don't want us to go back to London, as they are already looking forward to having cheap holidays here!"

My sentiments exactly, so luckily we were both in agreement, but what should we do next? The solution was to look for another place in the sun, but this time we were fairly positive that we knew where we wanted to live.

Coincidentally, not long after that, John had a phone call from a property company that he had spoken to previously, asking whether we were still looking for a new home in Spain. John explained the situation to them and they suggested that we might like to look at some other Spanish towns, where bargains could now be found due to the growing problems in the Spanish property market. Their local agent could pick us up in Jumilla and show us what was available. We agreed that we had nothing to lose and it would be foolish not to look at other options now that Residencial Santa Ana del Monte was no longer viable.

John and I stood outside the "Oficina de Turismo" (tourist office) at the appointed hour, watching out for the car driven by Chris, the local agent. We expected to see a man in a smart suit on his own, so when a car stopped near us and a couple got out we didn't take any notice of them, until a voice said: "John? Sue? I am Chris and this is my wife Susan."

First impressions were not good. I'm not saying that John and I were wearing our Sunday best clothes, but we were the clients after all and this rather scruffy-looking individual, with his crumpled suit and long straggly grey hair, and his wife, who looked as if she had come straight off the beaches of Benidorm, were not what we had been expecting. They were the professionals, but didn't look the part.

Worse was to come. I'm not a good traveller so whenever we have been on viewing trips in the past, I have sat in the front of the car with our agent, and John has uncomplainingly taken the back seat.

"I'd like to sit in the front as I'm not a good traveller," I said, moving toward the front of their car and not expecting any arguments.

"I have to sit in the front, as I get car sick," announced Susan, as she beat me to it. Hello? Who was the client here? I was too stunned by her bad manners to argue though.

To be quite frank, after that poor start, it was going to be difficult to impress me. The houses that we were shown were nowhere near as good as the Azucena that we had hoped to be living in at Santa Ana del Monte, and though we liked Rosales and Los Alcázares, where two of the properties were located, we found ourselves comparing both towns with Jumilla. As far as we were concerned Jumilla had everything that we were looking for and there was no comparison.

Chris and Susan had told us that they lived in a small Spanish pueblo, not that far from Jumilla, so we were a bit surprised when they took us to a British-run bar around lunch-time rather than a Spanish one. We fully expected them to suggest having lunch, which traditionally the agent pays for, though we did not have any objection to paying our share. When nothing was mentioned about having any food I nudged John and muttered, "Is there a menu here?"

John knows me well - I need to eat at regular intervals or I become very difficult - so he took the hint.

"Shall we have something to eat?" he suggested. Susan not surprisingly said she never had anything to eat at lunchtime - I had already taken a dislike to her and this reinforced my feelings - but luckily Chris said he could "manage a snack", so we were able to have some food.

Being perverse, I was glad that we hadn't found anything suitable, as I didn't feel this couple deserved getting any commission through us. On the way back to Jumilla, we drove through Pinoso, where they told us there was a very good café that they went to on a regular basis, so I made a mental note to avoid it in future! When we next went to Pinoso and walked past that café, we heard lots of British accents so decided not to stop there, as apart from the risk of meeting Chris and Susan again, we also suspected that prices would be higher than elsewhere.

After this experience we decided to concentrate our efforts on finding somewhere locally. Although property prices near the coast had been reduced and there were bargains to be found, we knew that we preferred being inland and we could still get more for our money there. Our initial decision to live in this area had been the right one, so all we had to do was find another property - preferably one that had been completed or at least had a roof on!

Looking Again

Our original agents, Stella and Mark, put us in touch with Nataliya at Don Piso in Jumilla, who did an amazing job, finding us a variety of new and old properties, all at reasonable prices. Now that we knew where we wanted to live all we had to do was find the right place. Two bedrooms, with a proper bathroom, plus a balcony so that we had some outdoor space and not overly expensive - that couldn't be too difficult, could it?

Unfortunately, many new Spanish properties only have a shower in the bathroom, which is not an option for two runners of advanced years who want to be able to soak their aching limbs after going for a run, so this ruled out some of the places that we looked at. We saw a couple of flats that we liked, but there wasn't a balcony or any outside space and one of the reasons we wanted to live here was to enjoy the good weather by sitting outside. One flat was over budget and far too large for the two of us anyway, though it would have been good when our family visited, whereas another one was fine apart from the size of the second bedroom, which was barely big enough for one single bed. Were we being too difficult? Would we ever find another property that would meet our specific requirements?

Luckily the answer was "yes" or - now that our Spanish was improving - "si". By chance, we were looking at properties in the window of Habitacasa when Manuel arrived back after his lunch break. We explained the problems with San José, which he said that he was aware of, and also that we were looking for somewhere else to buy in the area. He invited us into his office and told us about a new development that was close to completion. The price sounded right, there were two double bedrooms, a full bathroom and the all-important balcony - so we told him that we were definitely interested in seeing this apartment.

The apartment Manuel had on his books was part of a new block on the edge of town, set back from the main road so that it would be relatively peaceful, but still close to all of the amenities. The show flat was impressive, with good quality fittings and decent sized rooms. After all the heartache I felt excited again at the prospect of living somewhere like this and just hoped that John felt the same.

"What do you think?" I asked him. This wasn't the dream house we had seen two years earlier, but I knew that it was still somewhere I could live quite happily.

"Muy bien!" was his response. "I like the balcony and I could even keep a donkey there!"

Have I mentioned the donkey? When we first looked at living outside Jumilla, I suggested to John that, as non-drivers, we might want to buy bikes so we could get into town more quickly. He wasn't keen on the idea, as it had been many years since he last cycled, but proposed buying a donkey instead. I had hoped that he had given up on this idea!

Needless to say, John and I were wary about parting with any more money, however Manuel seemed very relaxed about the need to pay a deposit. He told us what we would have to do to get a mortgage, but reassured us that there was no rush, the "piso" (flat) that we wanted would be reserved for us and he gave us a list of the documents we needed to bring back to Spain the next time we visited the UK. We could then speak to the "chica" (girl) at the bank who he assured us spoke good English, and take things forward from there. This was reassuring, as Manuel's English was minimal, and although he had written down what he said we needed, we weren't 100% confident that we had understood everything he was saying.

So it looked like our dream was over, but we still had a promising future ahead of us in Jumilla. Would things go right for us this time? We were cautiously optimistic. John's son-in-law Jerry had seen the development at Santa Ana del Monte where we had originally planned to live and he had also seen the area where we were now talking about living and he made his views clear.

"Quite honestly, I can't see the two of you living in what will probably end up being a large ex-pat development in the middle of nowhere. I have seen you chatting to people in Jumilla and it is obvious that you enjoy being part of the local community. I think you will be far happier living in town."

We could only hope that Jerry was right.

CHAPTER TWELVE

A Day In The Life

Now that we had decided to make our new home in the town of Jumilla it was time to get to grips with more paperwork. So far, all we had were our NIE numbers, but we knew that we should sign on the padrón and also apply for "residencia" (residency). As John delights in pointing out, I am now over sixty so am officially a "pensionista" (pensioner), which meant that I would be entitled to free healthcare in Spain, once I had registered.

I phoned the Pension Service when we were on a trip back to London and they sent me the E121 forms with instructions on how to apply for healthcare. The only problem was that what they said I needed to do was not the same as what I needed to do in reality. This was Spain after all, where everything tends to take much longer than expected - however in this case we found the process a lot quicker and easier than we anticipated.

My letter from the Pension Service had informed me that all I needed to register on the padrón was my passport, but I was living in Spain and suspected that this wouldn't be enough. So when John and I went down to the ayuntamiento, we decided to take our NIE numbers as well, plus a copy of the rental contract showing the address where we were living. Needless to say we were right and copies of all these documents were needed in addition to our passports. We also needed to go to the nearby La Caixa bank to make a nominal payment for registering and take the receipt back to the ayuntamiento when we collected our certificates.

Much to our amazement it only took a couple of days for our certificates to be produced and we could now say that we were officially residing in the city of Jumilla. The next step for me, according to the Pension Service, was to apply for my "certificado de residencia" (certificate of residency) at the local police station, but the helpful police officer there insisted that I had to get it from the ayuntamiento and when we returned to the town hall they told us we didn't need anything else as our original certificate covered residency as well. Nothing here is straightforward. We decided to go to the local social security office (INSS) with my E121 forms, passport and certificado de empadronamiento and see what they had to say.

We struck lucky at the social security office. The man there spoke some English and assured me that I had all the necessary documents. It took him no more than ten minutes to enter my details on his computer, print out the form that I needed to take to the health centre and also produce my new EHIC card. He took the E121 forms from me, got me to sign, and then completed them and put them in an envelope addressed to DWP. That was it.

The following day I went down to the "centro de salud" (health centre) with the form, where they informed me that I should return first thing in the morning to register. As the centro de salud opens at 8am, I left John in bed the following morning. I went down to the health centre, took a ticket and sat waiting for my turn, then spent a few minutes in the office where they entered my details on the computer and printed off another form including the name of my doctor, who I was told spoke some English. I eventually returned home just before 9am to find John still in bed, and somewhat surprised by how quick I had been.

Becoming Residents

We spent some time on the internet researching what needed to be done to get residency and found the address of the nearest "Oficina de Extranjeros" (Foreigners Office), which was in Yecla. However when we went to Yecla we were told that, because we lived in Jumilla, we had to go to the office in Murcia, even though it was further away. The woman we spoke to was very helpful, and told us which documents we needed to take, plus the fact that we would need two passport-sized photos, and she gave us the application forms so we could complete them in advance.

It took us two trips to Murcia before we finally got our "certificados de residencia". On our first visit we queued up on a hot day for over an hour until we were near the front of the queue, only to find that the office was being closed for lunch, though apparently it would open again in the afternoon. I was reluctant to wait there without being sure that we would be seen that day, so went round to the other door to make further enquiries. It was fortunate that I did so, as the man there informed me that, because we were new applicants and didn't already have a resident's card, we wouldn't be able to see anybody in the afternoon, and would need to come back again in the morning.

We decided to get an early bus for our next visit and we arrived before the office opened, to find that there was an even longer queue than on the previous occasion. At least we reached the front of the queue before they closed for lunch this time, only to be told that we needed to go to a local bank to pay the registration fee. Fortunately, when we returned with the receipt, we were able to go straight into the office and were then directed to a different office, where we waited for the officer who dealt with "los ingleses" (the English) to return to his desk. It was worth the wait, as he printed off our certificates on the spot (my fear had been that we would be told to return for them on yet another day, as we had to do when we registered on the padrón!) We were now the proud owners of two certificados de residencia.

"Let's go and have a glass of wine to celebrate," John suggested. "After all, we are now officially Spanish residents."

On a recent visit to London, my friend Cathy had asked me, "What do you do all day?" Good question, Cathy, but difficult to answer, as no two days are the same in Jumilla.

What Do We Do All Day?

When you work for a living and have to travel by tube to your office in central London five days a week, you tend to know what you are going to do most days and it is hard not to feel bored by the prospect. We are now living in a Spanish town where we don't have to go to work, so we have a choice when we get up every morning. We could even stay in bed all day if we wished, though when the sun is shining it is no hardship to get out of your bed!

Some mornings John and I go for a run after breakfast, and on other days we go out walking. We meet Juana María for coffee twice a week and we now meet Nataliya on a regular basis too.

On Tuesday we look around our local market, which still has an amazing array of fresh fruit and vegetables, even in the winter months. Sometimes we bump into Jean and Charles, who live in nearby Fuente del Pino, as we are wandering around the market and on occasions we join them for a coffee in one of the local bars. We also meet up with other friends such as John and Annette for the occasional coffee or rare glass of wine.

I have been busy writing this book, which has re-awakened my enjoyment of writing, so I hope to continue describing my experiences of life in Spain even after I have completed it. I am also considering writing a crime novel, where a Spanish developer is stabbed in the back by unhappy ex-pats when he fails to deliver their new homes. Hmm - that could very well prove to be an international best-seller - I certainly know a lot of disgruntled property buyers who would buy it.

John has been writing his own guide to Jumilla, which involves researching all the local bars and restaurants. As he says, it is a tough job, but someone has to do it. Of course it will need updating on a regular basis, so I doubt if the research will ever be completed, but John's not complaining.

We signed up for free Spanish lessons, which we attend two evenings every week and which also means doing homework. I know, we are both in our sixties and have homework to do. How ridiculous is that? Our Spanish teacher María Luisa doesn't speak a word of English, so we now take our large Spanish dictionary to classes, in case we come across new words that we don't recognise.

Since we moved to Jumilla, we have attended many concerts in Teatro Vico, most of which are free, and various exhibitions in CAM Cultural, CajaMurcia Cultural and the local museums, which again are free. Most weeks, when we check our local paper Jumilla Siete Días, there is at least one new event in the "Agenda de la Semana" (weekly diary) at the back of the paper for us to look forward to during the following week.

We have also met up with various friends from the forum, when they have been visiting the area. Most of them are unlikely to be our neighbours now, but it is still good to meet people who, a year ago, we had expected to be living near at Residencial Santa Ana del

Monte. We hope that those friends who are now living in Spain near the coast will still venture inland from time to time, if only to stock up on Jumilla wine!

Then, of course, there are the fiestas.

August Fiestas

We had heard a lot about the "Fiesta de la Vendimia" (Wine Harvest Festival), which is celebrated in Jumilla every August, and it more than lived up to our expectations. There are actually several fiestas going on at the same time: the National Folklore Festival; Moors and Christians; the Fiesta of Jumilla's Patron Saint, La Virgen De La Asunción; plus the renowned Vendimia with its numerous competitions, celebrations and parades, culminating in the "Gran Cabalgata del Vino" procession on the final Saturday. During this last event, floats parade through the streets carrying barrels of wine, while the participants fill plastic bottles with wine, which they then direct at anybody within their range. I took lots of photos of the colourful procession, having to dart back on several occasions to avoid being soaked in red wine. Jumillanos certainly know how to party!

We discovered that there was going to be a race through the streets of Jumilla, as part of the celebrations in August. As runners, we were obviously keen to participate and were delighted to find out that, unlike the increasingly expensive races back in the UK, entry was free.

John had been feeling a few niggles in his calf while training for the race, but seemed OK on race day, so he was there on the start line. Unfortunately, half-way through the race, the problem returned. He decided to continue, partly through male pride and partly because he was wearing his Serpentine Running Club vest, but he had to walk on the last lap. In spite of this, he wasn't the last male to finish and he was rewarded with a trophy as the oldest runner to complete the race!

I was surprised to find that there were only twelve other runners in the women's race and looking around I suspected that I was the oldest female there by many years (John kindly confirmed this for me when he looked at the results). I was also pleased to find that I wasn't the last finisher, and as well as receiving an excellent "goody bag" for finishing, which contained a commemorative towel, a pair of running socks and a bottle of Jumilla wine (there's a surprise!) I was delighted to be presented with a trophy as 3rd veteran female.

While we were watching the Moors and Christians parade we recognised one of the participants, and waved to him. Before we could realise what he was planning, he came running up to John, handed him the blunderbuss he had been firing and indicated that he expected John to pull the trigger. I moved out of the way quickly, as the noise they make is extremely loud, only to be told that I had to fire it too! Next year we will have to make sure that we don't stand at the front of the crowds lining the street.

We are now looking forward to "Navidad" (Christmas) in Jumilla. My family will be here for their first Christmas in Spain and I am excited at the prospect of showing them round the town. We have reserved tickets for the Christmas concert in Teatro Vico on Boxing Day, which I hope the family will enjoy.

We have also booked a table at Restaurante Loreto for a family dinner on the Saturday night. Earlier that day, John and I plan to take part in the II Carrera Popular Navidena Jumillana (Jumilla's Christmas race), which starts outside Teatro Vico at 17.30 on Saturday. John is threatening to run the race in fancy dress: I suspect this is because he hopes to win a whole jamón!

Back to Cathy's question: what do we do all day in Jumilla? We are far too busy to be able to stop and think about it!

Sue Walker

CHAPTER THIRTEEN

Jumilla: Abierta Y Generosa

Jumilla's slogan is "abierta y generosa", and John and I definitely agree that it sums up our experiences of the town. People here have been very open and generous towards us.

One day during the fiestas in August, we heard a knock on our front door. We opened it to be greeted by our neighbour Asunción, who was holding a plate with cake on it, and another woman, who asked us if we spoke English.

"Yes. I *am* English," I said, slightly bemused by the question.

"My aunt thought you might be Swedish," was the puzzling response. "Today is her birthday and she wondered if you would like some of her birthday cake."

"Yes, of course. Gracias." We smiled at Asunción as we accepted the birthday cake from her. "Feliz cumpleaños!"

Swedish? Then we realised that she must have seen John's four blond-haired grandsons when they visited us and jumped to the wrong conclusion. She certainly knew that we weren't Spanish as, in spite of our Spanish lessons, we were still far from being fluent.

Yet More Fiestas

The villages near Jumilla often hold their own celebrations, as do the various districts within the town. We decided to go to the "Estampas Rurales" (where they demonstrate traditional crafts) in the village of Fuente del Pino, which Jean and Charles had told us about, however when we went to the bus station we discovered that the first bus wasn't due for a couple of hours.

I had seen some posters in town advertising a motorcycle rally, so we decided to investigate this in the meantime. It was easy to find, as we just followed the numerous motorbikes we spotted heading to where the rally was being held.

The organiser recognised us and called out "hola" when we arrived. After she had made various announcements, music started blaring out over the loudspeakers. We decided to have a cup of coffee in a nearby bar, where hopefully the music wouldn't be quite as deafening. As soon as we entered the bar we were given a couple of fritillas (pancakes), which had been cooked outside and were being handed out to the bikers, to enjoy with our coffees. Later, as we headed back to the bus station, we heard the roar of the motorbikes as they set off to visit one of the local bodegas. We hoped that the samples of wine at the wine tasting weren't going to be too generous, as they still had to return to Jumilla on their bikes.

We arrived in Fuente del Pino just in time to watch the parade. The procession included some young children on horses, a loose foal that luckily kept close to its mother's side and a cart on which a huge religious statue had been placed. Local people dressed in traditional costume followed behind, many of them singing as well as chatting while they strolled along.

The procession started on one side of the busy main road, and then slowly crossed to the other side, where the statue was paraded around the pueblo before eventually being carried into the local church. Luckily the Guardia Civil were there to stop the traffic, which waited patiently until everybody had safely crossed the road. In Spain, nobody seems to mind waiting if a fiesta is taking place.

A variety of stands had been set up in the College Gardens, demonstrating local artisan crafts, so we wandered around them, buying some hand-made soap and a brightly coloured necklace (for me, not John), as well as a couple of commemorative t-shirts. One of the women on the stand selling hand-made soaps spoke to us in English and we then discovered that although she now lives in Fuente del Pino she is actually French. I decided to practise my French on her, only to find that I kept confusing Spanish and French words and was speaking Franish to her - or should that be Frenish? I obviously knew more Spanish now than I had been aware of.

There were lots of stalls selling food and drinks, so we bought a book of tickets for ten euros, which allowed both of us to get plenty to eat, plus a bottle of wine between us. One good thing about moving to Spain has been that we can have a day out at very little cost, which is a bonus for impoverished pensioners.

Since moving to Jumilla we have found that there are very few weeks where nothing is happening in the town. Even when there isn't an official event, we often hear music playing, or hear loud bangs and see smoke at the end of the street, which indicates either that local musicians are practising for the next concert or fiesta, or that there is a wedding at the nearby church and fireworks are going off as part of the celebrations. Strangely enough, we have never seen fireworks on sale in the local shops, but somehow people get hold of them for important occasions such as weddings or Spain winning a vital football match.

Only last week, we heard a band playing, with several loud bangs at regular intervals, so John and I decided to see what was going on. We watched a small procession, led by a man brandishing a blunderbuss and setting off fire-crackers, so this time we made sure we didn't get too close to him. Later on that day we spotted the statue that had been carried in the parade, through the window of a building opposite La Tapa bar. We were being nosey and peering through the window, when an elderly lady spotted us and invited us to come in. We stood chatting to the group that we had seen earlier and before we left they generously invited us to join them the following Tuesday for "aperitivos, cerveza y vino" (aperitifs, beer and wine), as part of their fiesta week.

There have been numerous other examples of the people of Jumilla being "abierta y generosa" (open and generous), as the title of this chapter suggests.

We bumped into Juana María and her husband, Salvador, on our way to listen to a concert one evening. Juana María told us that the venue had been changed, as the weather was colder than usual and it was now being held indoors in the Mercado, so we walked there with them.

Afterwards, they asked us if we fancied going to Restaurante Reyes Católicos for a drink and some tapas, which we readily agreed to. We discovered that their idea of a drink and tapas was not the same as ours: we ended up sharing numerous plates of delicious tapas, a couple of bottles of wine and finally a huge plate of local pastries. Not that we were complaining - far from it! When the bill arrived, Salvador insisted on paying for us.

"We invited you," Juana María explained. "So we will pay for you. It's the custom."

A few weeks later we noticed posters advertising an evening of flamenco at one of the local bodegas, so we asked Juana María whether they would like to go with us. As we had invited them to join us on this occasion, we were able to insist on paying for their tickets.

The first weekend in December was a weekend of festivos (bank holidays), which we knew meant that most shops in Jumilla would be shut. We had already been caught out by a local festivo in August, when Consum and Mercadona had only been opened on

Saturday morning, and unfortunately we had decided to go shopping on Saturday afternoon. There had been no advance warning that this would happen, but luckily Aldi was open all day, so we didn't starve.

The bank holidays this time were on Saturday and Monday, so we fully expected that we would need to get all our shopping done on Friday, as the majority of shops in Jumilla close every Sunday. However, because it was a national holiday, there were notices in the supermarkets and we discovered that on this occasion the supermarkets were going to open on Sunday morning, so there was no danger of us going hungry.

The Lights Go Out

On Saturday evening, while dinner was cooking, our electricity went off without any warning. John went into the hallway to press the green button by the front door, but nothing happened.

"Have a word with the neighbours," John said. He drew back the curtains to give us some light and so he could look outside. "The street lights are on, so it may just be our building. It's a good job I brought all those candles back from London on our last visit, so that we would have them for Christmas. I'll light some, so we can see a bit better."

I tried a couple of our neighbours' doors, but there was no reply, so I went out into the street to see if there were any lights showing in our block. There were one or two lights, so it looked as if the problem was just with our apartment.

"Any joy?" John asked when I came back.

"No, people have obviously gone out for the evening but I could see a few lights, so it looks as if we are the only ones without electricity. I rang the bell at 3A where the caretaker lives and she isn't there."

"It's lucky that we've got a gas hob. Dinner is ready anyway, so let's eat now and try again later." John said. "After all, it's quite romantic dining by candle-light!"

"We're going to have to talk to each other too, as we won't be able to watch TV," was my response. "You wouldn't be quite so cheerful if there was football on TV tonight though, would you?"

"As long as we get our electricity back before the Champions League games are shown, I don't mind. Anyway, you can still use my laptop without electricity, so you'll be alright."

I tried the caretaker's door again later on and also in the morning, but there was still no reply. She must have gone away for the holiday weekend, so our only chance was to try ringing our landlord, but would he have his phone switched on? We didn't want to disturb him, but although there was a gas water heater which gave us hot water, as well as being able to use the gas hob to cook, we didn't really fancy two more days without any electricity.

Fortunately we were able to speak to Juan, our landlord, on the phone. He realised that we couldn't understand everything he was saying, so he asked us whether we were in our apartment and, when I said that we had gone out for a walk, what time we would be back there.

An hour later, and we heard the entry phone ring. Our landlord had arrived in person to help us. Juan showed us that there was another switch downstairs, which we had been unaware of and when he pushed the switch our electricity supply was restored. In spite of having had to drive into town from his country home on a bank holiday weekend, our landlord was his usual friendly self, and once he had explained how the different switches interacted he gave us a cheerful wave and drove off.

More and more people stop us in the street for a chat, to ask us how we are, and to discuss the weather. Sometimes we know exactly who we are talking to, and at other times we will recognise the face but aren't quite sure where we know them from. We have been fully accepted by the locals, even though I suspect they are bemused when they see the two British "jubilados" (retired people) out for their morning run. We feel very much at home in Jumilla and all we need to do is move into our own house and our search will finally be over. In the meantime, we are now actually living our dream, even though it isn't the one we initially envisaged.

New House – New Dream

It was several months since Manuel first showed us the piso where we hoped to be living soon and nothing much seemed to be happening. We were starting to get a bit anxious, although every time we saw Manuel he said that the documents we had given him were fine and there weren't any problems. We spoke to him last Wednesday and he told us that he had made an appointment for us with the "chica who speaks English" for Friday morning. At long last something was about to happen! I tried not to get too excited though after our previous let downs.

On Friday morning we met Manuel at his office at 8.30, which nowadays is an early start for us. He drove us into Orihuela and, much to our amusement, got lost in spite of (or maybe because of?) having GPS. Eventually we arrived at the offices of Tarancón, the developer, where we were introduced to one of the managers Evaristo who accompanied us to the bank.

Carmen, who was the English-speaking chica and who looked at least fifty, had a few questions for us: mainly for me, as I have three separate pensions as well as my state pension, which clearly had confused her. Finally, she informed us that the bank was happy to offer us a mortgage for our new flat and that she would send us the paperwork, with revised costs due to the lowering of the bank rate. The recent poor performance of the pound against the euro has been bad news for us, but at least we were going to see a slight benefit in the reduced mortgage payments.

On the way back to Tarancón's offices, I told Evaristo that I would like to be able to see inside what was now going to be our new home. He made a phone call and told us that it had been agreed with the site manager and Manuel would take us there when we returned to Jumilla.

We were half-way back to Jumilla when Manuel asked me if I would like a "cerveza", as we had time to spare before the site visit. On the assumption that I could have the drink of my choice rather than a beer, I said yes. I knew I didn't have to ask John whether he wanted one!

Manuel drew up in front of a restaurant near Blanca, which we had noticed before when the bus to Murcia had gone past it.

"I have always wanted to try this restaurant out," John commented as we entered the bar. "I'm glad that Manuel suggested stopping here."

Manuel asked us what we would like to drink, and when John and I both said "Vino", he replied "Bueno". He then ordered a bottle of wine, plus tortilla, olives, cheese and ham, which were served with bread. In spite of Manuel hardly speaking any English and our limited Spanish, we managed to have a good conversation while enjoying our tapas and wine.

When we reached Parque de las Avenidas, on the outskirts of Jumilla, we were met by the site manager who presented us with a couple of rather fetching blue hard hats. We had to walk up to the second floor as the lifts weren't yet in action and then through the front door and into our new home.

"The kitchen is a good size," John said as we started looking around the flat. "It's big enough for a kitchen table and chairs." I was already on my way to the salon-comedor (lounge-diner), so it wasn't until we got back to our rented apartment later on that I found out what I had missed in the kitchen.

"Manuel pointed out that there is a TV socket in the kitchen," John informed me. "He said that I will be able to watch Manchester United in there!" I have no problem with that, if it means I can watch what I want on another TV.

I loved the living area immediately, as not only was it a light spacious room, but also there were large windows leading onto the balcony, with views of the Sierra de Santa Ana del Monte. We also discovered when we all went out onto the balcony, that we could see El Carche, the highest mountain in the area, from there.

"So far we have got everything we have been looking for," I said to John. "Now all we have to do is check out the bathroom and bedrooms."

We had seen the plans of course, but now we were actually walking around our flat and could see for ourselves that we had two double bedrooms, plus - although the WC, bidet and washbasin weren't installed yet - the all-important bath was already in place.

"When will this be completed?" I asked as we walked back to the sales office.

"The roads, gardens and main building should be completed by the end of December, but your keys won't be handed over until February or March next year."

Just two or three months until we would be living in our own home in Spain - after five years of looking and nearly three years of waiting, it didn't sound too long to us.

John and I decided that this time the celebration deserved more than just a glass of wine.

"Let's go out for a meal to celebrate," he said as we walked back to the town centre. "Where do you fancy going?"

"Cafetería Monreal," I replied. "We can splash out on a nine euro menú del día there."

I forgot to mention that Manuel had presented us with a lottery ticket while we were in the restaurant, which unfortunately - when I checked it in the morning - wasn't a winner. However, now that at long last we have found our home in Spain, John and I feel as excited as if we had actually won the lottery.

This has been John's and my story which, after our various trials and tribulations, at last has a happy ending. In the next chapters you can read stories from other people who have made the move to Spain. I hope that between us we will inspire you to follow your own dream, and that by relating our stories we will help you avoid some of the problems we have experienced. At the end of the day though, as I am sure you will agree, it was well worth making the decision to retire to Spain. We are now living our dream.

CHAPTER FOURTEEN

Case Studies

John Jarvis is a fellow runner, who was also a member of Serpentine Running Club when he lived in London, and we had known him for many years before he decided to retire to Spain. This is John's story.

John Jarvis – Life In Nerja

"We bought our villa in Nerja in 1994, as a family holiday home in the first instance, but we have been living there most of the year since early 2005. While we were still resident in England we used a local agent to manage and let the property for us, and since retiring we have retained his services. For a small annual fee he deals with all legal and fiscal matters on our behalf, paying utility bills and any tax that is due. We consider this money well spent because, if you are not a fluent Spanish speaker, it is difficult to negotiate the minefield that is Spanish bureaucracy, and misunderstandings can occur and these can lead to your being fined, quite heavily, for not paying a local tax for example.

"During one of our early holidays I was introduced to a young man from Frigiliana (a nearby white village), whom everyone described as "mad Miguel" because he would run for hours in the mountains. When he heard that I too was a runner, he soon made arrangements for us to run together – and we ran together many times over the intervening years. He is as nimble as the mountain goats we see in the mountains, bounding along the rocky paths. One of our earliest runs was to the top of El Cielo and back – El Cielo is the highest peak in the area, 500ft higher than Ben Nevis – which we completed in four hours, door to door. It was a crisp clear autumn day and we could see across the Mediterranean to North Africa from the top, but it was very cold up there so we didn't linger long.

"Through Miguel I became a member of Nerja Atletismo, the local athletics club. The sports section of the ayuntamiento promotes running in most towns and it is through them that one can join a local club. Nerja Atletismo has a very active group of runners, of all ages, who made me very welcome even though I spoke poor Spanish. The younger members of the club practise their English on me and I practise my Spanish on the veterans, who speak no English at all. They all train regularly together, up to six nights a week. Each month we are given a fixed training programme. The club also encourages young people to take part in all field and track events, and they have won many trophies throughout Spain in the various age groups. One thing I have noticed is that there are no veteran ladies. There are young female runners, but as they get older they seem to give up running and go to the gym.

"One of my earliest runs with the club was a cross-country in the mountains near Malaga – 14 km straight uphill and 14 km down again. It was in November, but it was still hot and very gruelling. I remember passing people going up, only to be passed by them again on the way back down! At the end of the race the sponsors had provided refreshments for all the runners and my fellow competitors stood around eating large chunks of pork fat, blood sausage and ham, all washed down with beer – not quite the isotonic drinks and cereal bars I was used to in England! All the cross-country runs I have been involved in here in Spain have entailed running up a mountain and down again, on rocky mountain tracks.

"The club has a good record of winning trophies and I am pleased to say that I have added to their over-60s tally, mostly in half-marathons. These take place in various cities in southern Spain and generally involve a weekend visit, which means that wives are able to come and support the men. As the races are on Sundays we all go out for a meal together on the Saturday evening, often pasta suppers provided by the sponsors; on other occasions we descend en masse to a local restaurant, with everyone talking nineteen to the dozen, as only the Spanish can do. I remember when we went to Almería, we were going to dinner in the Directors' Suite in the local football club; the ladies were all dressed in their finery and one of the men took us on a short cut – which turned out to be through a hole in a fence and across the railway track!

"Every town has an annual fería (festival) which lasts for several days and involves lots of running or walking races through the streets of the town, for all ages, from five years to over sixty. At the end of each race every competitor receives a "goody bag", which generally contains local produce – I have on occasion had olive oil, oranges, lemons, sausage, tomatoes – and always a T-shirt and/or sweatshirt and a small trophy depicting scenes from the town. There is always some form of refreshment – roast pork rolls for example and free beer.

"In Nerja they also have the Christmas mile where the winner in each category receives a whole Serrano ham – even the youngest competitors, who struggle to carry off their prize. At the same event there is a walk for health, where the less fit members of the community walk the mile – but even this can be quite competitive as the ladies try to outpace their friends for the ham.

"We are fortunate in that the club has an active social life – they organise day-long walks on bank holidays, picnicking in the mountains, and we all get together for a dinner at Christmas time.

"One piece of advice I would give to anyone considering moving to Spain is to get to know the local people. This is easier through a running club because you have a common interest and you can meet people from all walks of life in the community – policemen, firemen, doctors, teachers, shopkeepers, plumbers etc. We have found that the Spanish people are very warm, welcoming and friendly, always ready to smile – say

"Hola!" as you pass people, they always respond in a friendly way."

The next story is Jacqui's. Unlike me, she and her husband are keen golfers, but hey, nobody is perfect (sorry, Jacqui!)

Jacqui Bott – Enjoying Good Health & Good Golf In San Juan De Los Terreros

"There are times in anyone's life when you want to run away and start again, but mostly it's a dream or a way to get over a bad day. For me it all started with the realisation that increasing health problems meant I could no longer continue to work at the level I had for a number of years. I was finding winters difficult as my arthritis got worse and as a new but avid golfer, winters in England were a continual struggle against the cold, the rain and the mud.

"As an accountant I had spent the last twenty years working in a large firm of estate agents in Sheffield and finally achieved my partnership in 2000. This brought its own stresses and about five years ago I had a nervous breakdown. Despite much help from doctors, therapists and work colleagues, I never felt I fully recovered and so, after many discussions with my husband about finishing work and going into semi-retirement, we agreed that I would finish at Christmas 2007 and get a part-time job locally where I could switch off when my working day was done.

"Over a bottle of wine one weekend later with some good friends the discussion turned to why we would stay in this country when somewhere warmer would be much more beneficial to my health and, before long, we were discussing a move to Spain.

"We had previously considered emigrating to California as we have some very good friends there and we loved the area and lifestyle, but our age was against us, we would have had to work fulltime to afford to be there and if we ever thought of retiring, we would have to return to the UK which was the last thing we wanted. So we accepted California was not for us at this stage in our lives.

"Southern Spain fitted so many of our criteria: it was warm all year round and predominantly dry, it was near enough to England to be able to get back quickly if we needed to and the cost of living meant, if we could buy a property outright, we could afford to live on our small pensions, albeit that they are subject to the exchange rate and so we had to make sure that when the rate is low we could still cover our bills. My husband has two grown up sons and we have a granddaughter who was just a few months old at the time, and so many discussions centred on moving away from them and our friends and how we would cope with the distance. We decided that we would be ok as there are enough methods of staying in touch with modern technology.

"We had been out to Murcia playing golf and decided that we would start our search there. After many sessions on the internet and several overseas property agents contacting us we decided on a small independently owned company in Preston that we were both comfortable to work with, and they arranged a couple of inspection trips to look at a variety of properties. They suggested we also take a look at Almería and when we first travelled down into the mountains we immediately fell in love with the area. We drove into San Juan de los Terreros and both felt we had found our new home.

"Terreros is a predominantly Spanish holiday village, with a small English contingent, most of whom have moved here in the last five years. Having lived in a city all my life I loved the idea of being by the sea, morning walks along the coast with our two dogs, coffee in a chiringuito (beach bar) looking out to sea whilst relaxing with a good book and a gorgeous mountain backdrop – it was idyllic. We talked about the change through the summer and how busy it would get but we decided we would accept this for the ten months of tranquillity. We found there was a new golf course nestled in the foot of the mountains less than ten minutes away and that clinched the decision for us: we would move to San Juan de los Terreros.

"So, we had a house to sell, dogs to organise passports for, decisions on what furniture to bring and what to leave, family and friends to see and say our goodbyes to, and we had to give notice to our workplaces. Sounds simple, but the whole lot took twelve months to organise and we finally closed the front door of our house in Sheffield for the last time in May 2008. We were lucky that everything went fairly smoothly but I think a lot was due to the research, planning and checking that we did. Research and planning is so time consuming but in the long run pays dividends.

"So, six months later we are well settled in our new life, and we love the area now as much as we did the first time we saw it, if not more. My health has significantly improved due to the warmer, drier climate and the lack of stress. We made sure we got involved with anything and everything we could when we first arrived and now have a good circle of friends that we see frequently, so we have not felt the loneliness we thought we might, having left all our family and friends behind. We make regular contact with people back in England and several have been out to visit us.

"When first moving out it makes sense to rent for six to twelve months, as you will come across places that you would have missed on inspection trips, and with so many properties available in every region there really isn't any need to rush into buying. We are lucky, we love where we are and wouldn't want to move elsewhere. Our days are filled with golf, dog walking and meeting up with friends. We love picking an unvisited area on the map, loading the dogs in the back of the car and going for a drive. As long as you can adopt the mañana attitude and not get worked up about delays, life can be good. Not speaking the language can be frustrating at times but there are so many ways of learning when you have moved here, that anyone wanting to learn can, without too much effort, but if you don't want to learn there are still ways of getting by.

"We still have chores to do - the cooking, cleaning, washing and shopping still need to be done - but having worked fulltime for thirty years, I am surprised to find I don't miss it at all. We both love our new lives here and have no regrets at moving. Would we move back to the UK? Never. We had always said if Spain didn't work for us there were too many other places to try before returning. That's why we sold everything and didn't leave a safety net – for us there was no going back."

Bob and Pauline also planned to buy at Residencial Santa Ana del Monte, so if all had gone well we would have been neighbours. Bob tells their story, which he has called "The Dream".

Bob and Pauline – The Dream

"It all started somewhere around January 2004. We, my wife and I, were running a large B & B or a small hotel, depends on which way you prefer to look at it, not too far from East Midlands airport and the lease on that business had a few years to run. We also owned our own house which we were renting out since we were living above the business, and that brought in a small income. Since the house was situated in a lovely hamlet only a mile or so away, a hamlet being a village that only has a church and no other amenities, we were able to run our business and keep tabs on our property quite easily.

"So one day - I think in the month of January - my wife said to me: "Where would you like to retire to in four or five years' time when our lease is up?" - me being of retirement age by then, although she would be some twelve years behind me.

"I thought about it for a minute, "I really don't know," I replied. "Perhaps somewhere like Wales. I do love the countryside and the cleaner air, and of course when we sell our home it will be cheaper to buy a house there which would leave us a bit more money over to go towards our retirement fund. What about you? Where would you like to retire to?"

"Her response took me totally by surprise. "Spain," she answered.

"Spain. Well you could have knocked me down with a feather. I had often thought myself about going to live abroad but thought Pauline would not go along with that, because of moving away from our families. At the end of the day though, Spain is merely a two and a half hour flight away, with some quite cheap flights as well.

"So I suddenly realised that we were both thinking on the same wavelength and also our families would love the comparatively cheap holidays in the sun. The dream had started.

"After talking for some days, that was it, the decision was made: Spain or bust. If of course the worst came to the worst, we could always come home, we both agreed.

"That started many months of doing our homework, most of which was done of course via the internet. We checked on prices of houses, what you get for your money, areas, the Spanish people and way of life, and just about everything you could possibly read about in the time that we had available to us. We wanted to live on the coast, near the sea and the hustle and bustle of things but also to be just far away enough from the tourists, like we were when we were on holiday. We wanted the best of both worlds: a little bit of peace and serenity but also a touch of night life as and when!

"Unfortunately, the properties near the coast were out of our price range, unless we compromised and accepted a much smaller property than we wanted, and that was something we were not prepared to do. We wanted space to breathe and also for our respective families when they came to visit us. Therefore, to buy the sort of property we were looking for in our price range, we knew we had to move inland, and so our search began.

"Eventually we found two or three properties within the Mazzaron area which we decided we would like to look at. Not wanting to go on an inspection trip with a developer and feel in some way committed, we decided to take a week's holiday and just have a look around at a few properties on our own. We booked our holiday which was for three weeks later.

"Then approximately ten days after that, in the middle of June 2004, on a very sunny and warm Sunday afternoon, we went to an "open" garden day in a local village called Thrumpton in Nottinghamshire, not far from where we lived. This was a once a year event that many villages do, whereby you pay an entrance fee of £1 per person, all of which goes to a charity and you are allowed to look around the gardens of various houses.

"We did in fact see some really attractive garden layouts, which were not only very nice to see but also gave you some tips or ideas for things you could do with your own garden. Now here is the crunch. We entered one front garden and looked around and then, as we approached the rear garden, we came upon an easel with a large picture of an Azucena house on it. It turned out that Linda and Steve who owned the house were one of many UK agents for San José who were selling Spanish properties off plan at Santa Ana del Monte, Jumilla. On further examination we realised that this property, standing on eighty-nine square metres and at a cost of €105,000 (the first price released on this property) was - compared to all the others we had seen - an absolute bargain. It shot to the top of our list.

"So, ten days later, we were on a flight out of East Midlands airport off to sunny Spain for our holiday and a look at those houses which we were interested in, leaving the Azucena to last. Leaving in our opinion the BEST to last.

"After looking at three other properties we then went to see the Azucena show house, which was at Albatera, another planned development being built by San José. At that stage there was nothing at all at Santa Ana del Monte, no not even a show house, just six and a half million acres of barren land. We approached the Azucena, looked at it from the outside and just looked at each other. Yes, absolutely, this WAS our dream house. We then entered and had a good look around, up stairs and down and almost simultaneously said to José, the representative who was showing us around: "We will take one." The dream was continuing.

"We left Spain for the UK a couple of days later like a couple of young lovers who had met for the first time. There is no other way of explaining it, or describing the feeling that we both had experienced. It really was like walking on air. Could this be true? Could this be happening? Was this a dream coming true? Yes, it really was like love at first sight. We LOVED the Azucena.

"Within the next few weeks we had paid our 30% deposit and had signed the contract which stated that our property would be completed by 30th May 2005. This meant we would have a holiday home for two to three years before we eventually retired.

"We had read about bank guarantees on the internet, which means the bank covers your deposit in the *unlikely* event of your house not being built on time or the developer going bust. So we asked our agent for one, since we knew that we were supposed to be given one by law. We were told by our agent that we were the first people to ask for a bank guarantee and that San José had been going for some thirty years, so we didn't need one.

"We weren't accepting that. "Really?" we replied. "Well we still want one." To be honest and fair, after another couple of phone calls to the agent and about two months, we received one in the post. We were happy.

"So with the deposit paid, the contract signed and our bank guarantee in our possession, all that was left to do was to wait for our Azucena to be built the following year. So we waited and waited and waited and waited... As the years slipped by it was excuse after excuse. Was our dream slipping away from us? Would there be a happy ending?

"Well, we did retire in December 2007, sold the remainder of our B & B lease and also our house, and rented a house in Nottingham for six months while we tied up loose ends. We then moved to Spain in May 2008 and rented an apartment, only for San José and Herrada del Tollo, our developers, to go into voluntary administration after one week of us arriving. Our original dream was shattered. Is that the end of our story? Not quite.

"A new dream is born! We were fortunate enough to have enough money to buy a nice house, better in our opinion than the Azucena, seven to eight minutes drive from the beach, which had been our original intention though we hadn't been able to afford it four years ago. Now, in a depressed housing market four years on we can afford that and still have a retirement fund which should last us many years. If and when we get our deposit back off our bank guarantee, that should last through most of our remaining years on this earth. God willing.

"Will we stay in Spain and never permanently return to the UK? Well, one can never say never, but the chances are good that we will. We love the country with its good points and its faults, the people, the way of life and also the weather. It's the whole package that makes retirement here more attractive to us than the UK, as much as we love England. Spain is a lovely country with good and interesting food and of course more than affordable copious amounts of vino. A country which is family orientated and looks after and respects its older generation. There is not much more one can ask of a people.

"Any regrets? Just the one and that is that maybe not everyone who has struggled to make a new life in Spain will be as fortunate as we have been. We just hope that most will and, anyway, wish all those ex-pats the best of luck in the world. For us, our dream is now a reality."

I first came across Linda (GAL) on the owners' forum, and we then had the pleasure of meeting her and her husband (known as the Laird of Lochaber) at the get-together in Torquay. No doubt we will still meet up from time to time to swap stories about our different experiences of living here in Spain.

Linda – from Benidorm to San Miguel

"My name is Linda, known to everyone as GAL, standing for Great Auntie Linda. More of that later. It is December 13th and a bright sunny morning has dawned here on the outskirts of San Miguel de Salinas. You wouldn't expect to see the sea from 5km inland, but we live at the top of the hill and it is so bright I can't see the sea for the reflection on the water.

"So why did I decide on Spain? Some thirty years ago I came on a trip to Benidorm: it was not as it is today and, being twenty-one at the time, I didn't see much of it anyway. Then twenty-seven years later my sister bought an apartment in La Vila Joyosa, the next town to Benidorm and we were allowed to use it for holidays. This started our passion with what would become our new homeland.

"Why Spain? Apparently the Costa Blanca has the best health in Europe and there is always the sun. I just love it. Nearly every day there is sunshine: it warms the old bones. Just what I came for.

"Dave and I had been looking for four years, from Valencia to Marbella and inland and were sure Jumilla was the place for us. How wrong we were.

"The move was done with military precision - well we were both SNCOs in the Army when we met. Everything went well and we arrived at Santander then drove through Spain to our first night's stop at the Hotel La Zenia. Funny, it was the second time we had stayed there; the first was on our inspection trip.

"I came to Spain to retire but have not stopped working since I came here. I realised after three weeks that, having been active for fifty-nine years, I couldn't just sit and soak up the sun. I needed to get out and meet people, so I applied for a job as a holiday let cleaner. There were 250 applicants and one job - says it all, eh! No brain work is needed, the pay is small but it allows me to dine out regularly, very different from the UK.

"I wouldn't have been in this position if only our builder San José had been up front with us before we left the shores of the UK. Like Sue and John, plus many other couples and families, Dave and I had bought an off-plan property at Residencial Santa Ana del Monte near Jumilla. We had left for Spain with the expectation of moving into our new home later that year and were not prepared for the shock to come.

"We were out of contract by some fifteen months, so asked San José to accommodate us. They offered us a second floor two-bedroom apartment above their offices in La Zenia, South Costa Blanca. We were not to be alone there, as four other sets of people we had met were given the same option. We all arrived between January and April 2008. There were people from other developments living there too. Then on 6th May San José went into voluntary administration: they had let us make life changing decisions without even a thought for their clients.

"At this point we made a decision that we still wanted a home in Spain so we went ahead, used the other half of our house payment and found a home here in San Miguel de Salinas. In a way I feel I have been let off as Jumilla would not have been right for me, on a complex which would have taken up to ten years to complete, we would have been on a building site for all that time.

"In the UK I worked full time as Estate Manager of a sixty-four apartment complex which, had I known at the time, was to set me up for the other job I have here in Spain. We moved into our new home on a small complex of thirty-six houses at the end of September. It is seven years old and had been used as a holiday home by an old man, Ted, who was still present when we moved in: not in body but in spirit. He would bang and crash about at around 4am, waking us up.

"We had been here for a month and went to the ayuntamiento to change our padrón, only to be told that there was a small problem. Ted was still on the padrón, although he had been dead for five years. We contacted our estate agent, who got us a copy of the death certificate from the UK, and we then had him removed, I came home and told Ted he was welcome to come here but no longer owned this house. Since then the noises have stopped.

"The AGM for our urbanisation was held just four weeks after we completed and we were invited by the then President to attend. The meeting went as meetings go, with the exception of one thing: the President resigned due to family reasons. No one volunteered so my husband Dave told me to volunteer. I was voted in unanimously, after living here for just four weeks. I agreed to put myself forward as I know I will be able to move the urbanisation on and do a good job. What a start to retirement, eh!

"Now to explain "GAL". When I first met the people whom I was to live with at Santa Ana del Monte, I only had a niece so was known as plain old Auntie Linda. That is some three years ago now and my only niece Kyja has given me the opportunity to become a great aunt on two occasions: the first was Alexander, who at two is a real boy - those with children will know what I mean by this. Talisa was expected before we moved to Spain but had other ideas, arriving just five days after our move. I think she wanted us to go back to the UK to see her.

"Tips for anyone thinking of buying: do a recce to make sure it is where you want to be. I would never buy off plan again, even for a bargain.

"At present it is a buyer's market here in Spain. When we looked three years ago we couldn't afford to live near the coast and now that is exactly where we are. This area has lots to do and see, and it is only one and a half hour's drive from Benidorm, where my story began all those years ago.

"The only thing that I would have done differently is keep my money in my pocket until I had a roof over my head."

Good advice from Great Auntie Linda, who is clearly making the most of her new life in Spain.

Sue Walker

CHAPTER FIFTEEN

Case Studies From The Campo

Many people believe that by buying a ruin and doing it up they will get their dream home. Having visited David and Louise's lovely home, we agree that the end result can be fantastic, but it doesn't necessarily happen overnight.

David and Louise – Nearly Ten Years To Transform Their "Ruin"

"David and I live in a small pueblo outside of Jumilla. Or in the "campo", which is what the locals call the countryside. Our story is probably slightly different to most ex-pats living here, as it evolved rather than being pre-planned. We have learnt much and often look back at how green we were and how much we did not know about Spain and its people. We bought here nine years ago and it has been, and continues to be, a big adventure.

"When we met we were both in our late forties. A couple of years later we married and, as we were living in my small flat in North West London, I thought it might be a good idea to find a place to call our own. We looked at properties around London, but soon concluded that we were going to have to mortgage ourselves to the hilt for a third bedroom and a small garden, which seemed crazy.

"I had lived in Africa during my twenties and had always thought that I would like to live abroad once I retired. At this time I was not thinking about retirement but for some reason I suggested that we should look for a house abroad.

"Italy was our first choice, however the cost of living there ruled it out, so we decided to look in Spain. We booked an out of season villa in Oliva for a week and set off for a recce.

"We had no preconceived ideas of what we wanted. We had £15,000 which meant we could afford around £80,000 with a mortgage. Prior to our trip I made several appointments with estate agents via the internet, explaining our requirements and our budget.

"By day three we had still not viewed any properties. At the time I thought this was ludicrous; nowadays I understand why. They would give us a map, saying go and look at the area and then come back. It takes hours to drive around, through country roads, dirt tracks and the like and who could afford, in the business sense, to spend days with a couple who may not buy anything?

"The day before we left for our trip, I had read a small lineage advert for Country Homes based in Pinoso, west of Alicante. So on day four, fed up with the agents we had seen, I rang and said we were on our way, not realising how far Pinoso was from Oliva. Nearly two hours later we met the agents and off we went. For four hours we drove round mountains, up hill and down dale but we could not see anything that remotely clicked, so to speak.

"We stopped for lunch in a small place called Encebras, and I remember thinking, "It's like a ghost town", before opening the door to the small restaurant, which was heaving with people and life. Old men playing dominoes, children running around: the noise was deafening. You could buy wine from the Bodega over the road for a few pesetas from the tap on the barrel. At that time you could count the number of ex-pats living in the area on one hand. This was a farming community and foreigners were a novelty and "rich".

"During lunch, which took almost four hours, we proceeded to get quite merry and that's putting it mildly. The agent asked if we liked anything, I said "no", so she asked what we were looking for. I said I really did not know but none of the rooms in the houses that we had seen were big enough, all had been modernised by the Spanish residents and they were like something out of the 70s.

"She nodded. "I think I have just the thing for you," she said. So we very merrily (literally) trotted off to view "our ideal house".

"We recently looked at a video we made of the house the day we bought it. We were astonished. "Did we *really* buy that?" - we must have been mad! It was a wreck: the water wasn't connected, there was electricity of sorts, birds' nests and holes in the roof, but I knew the minute I walked through the door that this was it.

"David was horrified until he found out the price. It had not been lived in for 30 years but had many things going for it, not least the fact that we could buy it for £18,000. This meant no mortgage and pay as you go. I realised we had made a mistake earlier in defining how much we could afford to pay. It was time to go on another bar crawl: we eventually left at 1am to return to Oliva and to this day I do not know how we made it.

"Early the next morning we discussed the property and realised that we had not seen a toilet anywhere. We drove back to look around without agents and we broke in. The toilet was in the overgrown back yard and was a hole in the floor. We didn't know if we could do everything that needed doing but decided that it would not be the end of the world to lose £18,000, so we bought a 512 square metre wreck. Today we feel that the house chose us, not the other way round. We knew nothing about the area or buying in Spain. We just did it.

"The next thing was to get a local builder to give us an estimate for the first phase of the work. We didn't intend to do the building work ourselves though I wanted to do the decoration. The agent told us that labour was cheap and we estimated three years start to finish. How naive was that?

"The estimate was £140,000 - and that was just the first phase - out of the question! The agent said she could arrange the work for a new roof and that it would cost

£3,000 and take around four weeks. Nobody would sign a contract so we agreed to pay two men an hourly rate. It took three months and cost us just over £12,000. This was when we first realised that we could not trust anyone to tell us the truth. We believed we were being duped, but we were in the UK so it was difficult to prove.

"Now we had to roll our sleeves up, put the overalls on and get stuck in ourselves. We came out weekends and holidays and worked from early morning to late at night. The house looked ten times worse six months after we bought it, as we dug trenches to put in drainage and water, and channelled out for electrics. Materials were cheap and we were doing OK apart from the language. We made what is now the hall reasonably habitable and camped in it for what turned out to be nearly four years.

"We tried to learn Spanish using computer courses, but we worked long hours in the UK and we were too tired, however good our intentions were. We picked up quite a bit when we were in Spain though, from our Spanish neighbours.

"We consider ourselves very lucky, in so much as we were a novelty to the Spanish people in our pueblo. They did not understand why we would want to come to this place when we came from a rich country like the UK, but they wanted to help us to integrate.

"On one occasion I opened the door to a group of about ten Spaniards, all babbling and pushing. Eventually, in mostly sign language, we worked out that they wanted to invite us to the local fiesta. Very endearing. Now I realise they had probably spent hours in the local bar figuring it out and trying to elect someone to do the talking.

"On other occasions they would turn up at 11.00 in the morning and push us out of our own front door, us in overalls and covered in cement, and take us on guided tours of the area, visiting bodegas and meeting cousins, aunts, uncles, etc. Everyone between Jumilla and Pinoso is related in some way it seems. We would be gone for five or six hours and the concrete set hard in the barrow. We used to get stressed because we had not achieved our goals for the day. It took many months to see how futile that was and how valuable those excursions were. They could not understand us nor we them but we had such fun.

"I remember Diego in the builders' yard doing "sitting on the toilet" impressions the first time we went to buy a toilet. Also trying to get the man on the JCB, who seemed to be digging a hole to Middle Earth, to understand that we were putting in a septic tank, which he had never seen before. I used a shoe box and a spirit level to demonstrate that it needed to be flat at the bottom, while he scratched his head and thought I was "loco".

"Nowadays it's different. They have nicknamed David Kofi Annan and our house is the United Nations. We spend hours translating and sorting issues for both ex-pats and Spaniards from assorted local pueblos. However we didn't really get to grips with the language until we moved here on a permanent basis. David's comprehension is better than mine, I write and read better than he does, so between us we manage fine.

"We had been travelling backwards and forwards for about two years. Gradually it became evident, especially as the house was beginning to take shape and we knew we could achieve what we had set out to do, that we preferred the life in our pueblo. We had time for each other and we had so much fun. Our time was our own, not to mention the sunshine and the cheap cost of living (that was before the Euro). It was the complete opposite to our lives in the UK.

"It would take us weeks to adjust when we got back to the UK. The demands on us were wearing us down, as we both worked long hours. David had owned a Metal Fabrication business for thirty years but it was becoming difficult with the traffic, congestion charges, rents, rates and overheads. Stress was taking its toll. I was starting to look to the future and could not see a bright one for us in retirement.

"David's best friend, who was a Bank Manager, told us that a company had bought some land near Jumilla to build a golf course. I managed to discover who it was and we started thinking this could be a way of moving over for good. We could start a business selling golf packages to golfing couples, perhaps to those who wanted midweek breaks rather than a week's holiday. If we sold the flat we could buy a house on the course, rent that out and we would have an income and an interest. David lost most of his pension in the last financial crisis and mine is virtually non-existent because I had brought up children. The Spanish house was still a wreck but we thought if we worked on it full time we could finish it to coincide with the opening of the golf course. A door to a new future was opening up for us. We sold the flat, dealt with much flak from the family, closed David's business and moved.

"We had thought we could spend three days a week doing paid work, David making rejas (security bars) and other metal work and me painting it, spend three days continuing to work on the house, and have a day off. By now there were many ex-pats moving here. Some attempted to make a living working as estate agents selling property and land. In town the housing was mostly apartments; in the campo mostly old houses. A huge market sprang up for new build houses because there weren't any. Prices were still good but were rising, and with it everything else, over a very short period of time. This had been followed by the Euro replacing the Peseta. We now needed to find paid work five days a week, just spending weekends on the house.

"David found it difficult to adjust as he had never lived outside the UK. He hated not being able to speak the language and after six months we considered going back. We did not, and with the help of Spanish friends we have never looked back. The golf course has not materialised and it is possible we will lose our deposit on the house there. Our biggest fear now is that without the planned expansion of Jumilla together with its golf course, our future here is at risk as we have no way of making a living in retirement.

"Our house is still not finished. We do not go flat out any more. We have about another two years' work: in all it will have taken ten years to complete. It's impossible to establish what it has cost us financially, but we have had a wonderful, adventurous and fulfilling time."

What an inspiring story! We can only hope that David and Louise are able to spend their retirement enjoying the beautiful home that they have created.

John and Annette also live in the Campo, between Jumilla where we live and Pinoso. They are enjoying living in a small community, where they have been welcomed by their Spanish neighbours. John tells us about his new life in Spain.

John – From Queuing In The Army To Queuing At The Social Security Office In Jumilla

"We decided to live in Spain rather than other countries because it is easier and cheaper for the kids and grandchildren to visit us, and if there are any problems at home it is also easier and cheaper for us to fly back. When my Dad became seriously ill I managed to get back in time to see him, which was fortunate as he died just a few days later.

"The first time we had a holiday in Spain we fell in love with the place and decided we wanted to move there once I retired from the Army.

"We looked at properties in inland Almería first but didn't find anything that met our requirements, then we had a look further north near Girona, which proved to be very expensive, even though we weren't looking to live near the coast. Finally we drove around inland areas near Málaga, where at last we found a village that we really loved but unfortunately there weren't any properties available and, to be honest, for what you were getting, it was also very expensive.

"We decided the next area to investigate should be somewhere in between, so Annette did some research on the internet before we visited Spain again. We rang an estate agent in Pinoso, which Annette had found, then booked a hotel in Alicante, driving up each day to view the properties the estate agent had arranged for us to see. The estate agent was very helpful, checking at each stage that we understood and translating everything for us. Through her we found the house where we are now living.

"To be quite honest, we were very naïve: we didn't use a solicitor and we let the estate agent guide us all the way. Having heard many horror stories since, we realise how lucky we were that she was very professional and attentive to our needs and that everything went so smoothly. As we get older, we will eventually reach the stage where we will need to move closer to town or even buy somewhere in town and we will definitely use the same estate agents again. Karen has become a friend of the family and a constant source of information and help ever since.

"For those interested, we used: 'Inmopinos' Estate Agent in Pinoso. English is spoken, which helps make the process smoother, even if you do speak some Spanish.

"We completed the purchase in May 2006 and prepared for our move to Spain. Annette had been busy running four bars and a civilian restaurant within an Army camp, so she was looking forward to a change of pace, as was I after thirty-one years in the Army.

"Our main concern about moving to Spain was our two dogs, a Retriever and a Yorkie, who would have to fly in the hold of the plane. We tried to get them used to the containers they would travel in beforehand, putting biscuits inside to tempt them in, but Baron the Retriever was having none of it.

"We arrived at Gatwick airport at the ridiculous hour of 3am, assembled the containers in the departure lounge and, to our amazement, Baron calmly walked into his container and lay down! We had to sit with the dogs until just before we were due to depart and hand them into cargo.

"As soon as we landed at Alicante our first thoughts were for the dogs, but we had to get our cases before going to find them in the cargo area. As we stood by the conveyer belt we heard people laughing and, to our amazement, we saw the containers holding Baron and George coming round on the conveyor belt. Luckily the wheels had been removed, but I still needed a couple of strong men to help me lift Baron's container, which with him inside was over 60kg, down to the ground. We let the dogs out to have some water, after which they went back into their containers without having to be told: so much for our worries.

"I had started taking Spanish lessons at night school before we left the UK and have continued having lessons on a weekly basis since arriving but even after living here for over two years, I still find at times that people talk far too quickly. Once they realise I speak some Spanish they talk more rapidly, and even when I ask them to speak more slowly, they do so for a few seconds then forget. Annette still doesn't speak very much Spanish, however she seems to know instinctively what people are saying to her (it's a 'woman thing' I am told!) but between us we get by pretty well.

"During the fruit harvest it is not uncommon for us to have a knock on the door around 11pm, when the locals have finished work, and to be presented with a case of fruit - oranges, almonds, grapes, peaches or whatever is being harvested at the time. However we can only eat so much fruit, so Annette has taken to making a *lot* of jam and cakes that we deliver back to the neighbours and friends.

"There are times when we are planning to go out for the evening, however we pass one of the neighbour's houses and they spot us and insist on inviting us in for some food and drink. By the time we manage to leave (usually around 01:30 – 02:00) we realise it is far too late to go for our intended night out. However we probably have had a better night, without cost. The Spanish people welcome you and take you into their families wholeheartedly: 'mi casa es tu casa' (my house is your house).

"The only real problem we have had is that, because we are still in our fifties, we aren't entitled to free medical treatment in Spain, now that our E106s have run out. We took out private medical insurance, however when Annette needed treatment the company refused to pay out because, "it was already in your body". Ridiculous though that seems, they also said that if she had had cancer, as an example, she wouldn't be covered, so I would advise anybody under retirement age to examine medical insurance policies very carefully before paying out a lot of money.

"Annette loves absolutely everything about her new life here in Spain. The only thing that annoys her is if she is sitting in a bar listening to other Brits criticising Spain. She has to bite her tongue, though she wants to ask them, "Why are you here, then?"

"I agree with her. If you are living in inland Spain you need to integrate. It's no use expecting the Spanish to speak English, why should they? If you think you are going to be ripped off, which can happen, look around and price things first, then you will have a rough idea what you should be charged and can make sure you don't pay over the odds.

"I think what I like most about living here is the pace of life. OK, you sometimes have to wait for ages in a queue, only to be told that you have to come back another day, but I used to be in the Army: I'm used to queuing!

"One final word of advice: if you are thinking of moving to Spain, do your homework, rent first to see if you really do like it and spend time in the UK doing at least a basic Spanish course!"

CHAPTER SIXTEEN

Tips & Further Information

Before You Start Searching For A Home In The Sun

- Draw up a checklist of what are you looking for in your new country. Use your head as well as your heart when deciding which country you intend moving to and which area(s) you will visit in your search for a new home.
- Do as much research as possible before you move, especially if you plan to work for yourself or need to find employment to cover your living expenses.
- If possible, rent first before selling any property in the UK and buying abroad.
- If you have only seen an area in the summer holidays visit it in the winter months and vice versa.

Viewing Trips

- Before booking a viewing trip, ensure that you won't be part of a group.
- Make sure that the agent knows exactly what you want, which means of course making sure that *you* know exactly what you want.
- If there is no flexibility in your budget let the agent know, and insist that it will be a waste of both your time and theirs if you are taken to look at any properties above your upper limit.

- Give marks out of ten to every property that you look at, and if there are two of you do this independently.
- Don't be pressurised by overly-keen agents into making a decision. Remember the cautionary tales that you have read previously.

Making The Decision

- Research the different regions to discover potential places for you to live in. Remember that this is a very personal decision. John and I have decided to buy inland in the north-east of Murcia, but although we think it is beautiful here, you may visit the area and hate it.
- Don't rely on the old favourites, where you have enjoyed holidays in the sun in the past. Why not look at the Costa Verde in northern Spain, especially if you don't want endless days of sunshine? The Costa del Luz, close to southern Portugal, is still reasonably priced if you want the south but can't afford Costa del Sol prices. Explore inland Spain before deciding to settle on the coast, as you may be pleasantly surprised.
- Be practical and don't have any illusions. We speak a bit of Spanish, but not enough to be sure of finding a local job in the area where we will be living. However we are not relying on earning an income to be able to survive in Spain. If you are looking for work in an ex-pat area, you will be competing with other ex-pats and English speaking Spaniards. Ideally you should

have at least one year's money to support yourselves if you are looking for work.

- When you have found a place that you absolutely love, think of all the disadvantages as well as the advantages before handing over the deposit. Can't think of any? Are you sure? If the answer is yes, then clearly you have found your ideal new home.

- Draw up a checklist of "must haves", "nice to haves" and "no ways". Nobody else can do this for you, as only you know your priorities. Don't compromise on the "must haves", be flexible over the "nice to haves" and don't be too rigid about the "no ways".

- Don't rush your decision. If you were buying a property in the UK you wouldn't sign any papers until you were sure that everything was OK and that you were making the right decision. Be just as careful before signing papers for a property abroad and remember the golden rule: don't part with your money until you have a bank guarantee. Also be aware that even bank guarantees aren't 100% watertight.

- If you are planning to buy a permanent new home in Spain, the economic climate may prove helpful, as you don't have to worry so much about whether prices will increase or decrease in the same way that an investor has to, however you still need to be realistic about what you can afford to buy. When times are tough, the vendor is more likely to accept a reduced offer, so use it to your advantage

- Get a good independent lawyer, preferably one recommended by somebody who has used their services, but don't go on the recommendation of the developer, vendor or agent.
- Once you have made your decision you haven't finished the process. You have only just started out on your journey, and although it is going to be an exciting voyage and you are longing to get to your destination, be prepared for traffic jams, the occasional by-pass and possibly some unexpected detours.

Beating The Credit Crunch

As we are now both retired, we have been looking at ways to save money, even though living costs in Spain are far more reasonable than back in London.

- We have signed up for loyalty cards with both Consum and Día. Every month I get a cheque back from Consum, which I use as part payment towards my next shopping bill. At Día, there are many special offers in store for holders of a Día card, plus whenever we shop there we get vouchers with our till receipt, which gives further discounts off a range of products over the month.
- Go to your local pescaderia for your fish, as prices are lower than in the supermarkets, and the fish comes straight from the nearest fishing port. Most fish in our nearest shop costs us only two euros a kilo, and we often get a couple of extra ones thrown in after our fish has been weighed.

- Look out for produce being sold in people's garages. We buy fresh eggs and potatoes at a garage near us, which are fresher and tastier than those sold in the supermarkets, plus far cheaper of course.
- As in the UK, it pays to shop around. Although many products in Mercadona are more expensive than the other supermarkets, we can buy fresh milk there a lot cheaper than elsewhere.
- Visit your local bodegas for wine, as you can usually sample some first, and also it will cost you less. You can even take a plastic bottle to fill up with vino de mesa (table wine)!
- The local market is another place to visit on a regular basis, for a wide selection of fresh fruit and vegetables at reasonable prices, as well as many other products.
- Get to know your local shopkeepers. We often pop into the Electrical and Home shop at the top of our street, and unless an item appears to be a bargain, we will check similar shops before deciding where to buy it. On a couple of occasions when we have spent money there, the owner has given us a "regalo": the first time it was a wooden plate and last time it was a wooden spatula. Both presents have proved useful.
- Look through your local paper for special events and free offers. We regularly go to the theatre for free or cheap concerts, which we have spotted in the weekly paper, plus we found out that the province of Murcia was offering free bus travel

on Sundays throughout December - ideal for Christmas shopping trips.

- If you are buying several large electrical items try negotiating a discount for cash, just as you would do in the UK.

- Many local councils provide free Spanish lessons, so take advantage of them.

Dining Out In Spain

- If you are on a budget eat out like the locals do, having a menú del día at lunchtime. The advantage is that your meal and drink will usually only cost between eight and ten euros, which may even include a bottle of wine. One of our favourite places for menu del día is Bar Paraiso, where for eight euros we have salad, followed by three courses, bread, a bottle of la casera (lemonade), a carafe (or two) of wine and finally coffee. We don't need to eat much in the evening after dining there, so another saving.

- Vegetarians need to take care when eating out in Spain, which I have to say isn't really geared up to vegetarians, especially inland. Most salads will include tuna, so if you are asking for a mixed salad, check that it doesn't include any meat or fish. Also, many starters sound as if they are suitable but you may order a plate of green beans, double check that it is "sin carne" (without any meat) and then discover when it arrives that it contains ham. Yes, that happened to me on one occasion. "Carne" is taken to mean red meat only, so you need to be sure that your dish doesn't include "pollo" (chicken) or "jamón" (ham) either. If the menu doesn't appear to contain any suitable dishes it is always worth asking if they can prepare something for you. Many Spanish restaurants are more than happy to accommodate you and prepare some grilled vegetables, tortilla or other suitable dish.

- Apart from a few establishments on the coast, most Spanish restaurants serve meals at the traditional times, so you are unlikely to get menú del día before two o'clock, or cena (dinner) before nine o'clock. Of course if you are hungry and can't wait until then, tapas will always be available.
- Be aware that Spanish measures are usually huge, so if you are counting units of alcohol, one drink will always be more than one unit.
- Never drink and drive in Spain, as the limits are lower than in the UK (plus see the point above).

Health In Spain

- If one or both of you already receives a state pension contact the International Pension Centre in the UK for form S1 (formerly E121), which allows you to register for free healthcare in Spain. Similarly, if you have been in full employment prior to moving to Spain but are below state pension age, you may be entitled to free healthcare for a short time after moving. Ask HM Revenue & Customs to send you form

S1 (formerly E106) in this instance. As things can change (when I moved to Spain I completed form E121) I recommend checking the website below for the latest up-to-date information: *www.ukinspain.fco.gov.uk/en/help-for-british-nationals/living-in-spain/pensions-benefits/healthcare/*

- If you are planning to work for yourself be aware that you will need to make social security payments in order to get free healthcare and this will cost you around 250 euros a month at the time of writing. Check the Spanish Social Security website for the latest rates and further details: *www.seg-social.es/Internet_6/index.htm*

- If you are employed, your employer will make social security contributions, but do not rely on finding employment immediately.

- Private medical insurance in Spain will not be cheap if you are close to retirement age, so make sure that you look into the cost of this in advance and remember to read the small print to make sure what the scheme covers.

Cars in Spain

- As a non-driver I cannot advise drivers, other than to suggest that you research the options for taking your own car to Spain or buying when you get there, as I know it is not straightforward. You also need to be aware of Spanish law for motorists, including the items that you must always have in your car.

- As a pedestrian, I have noticed the following tendencies of Spanish drivers: they like to park near to or even on pedestrian crossings; they don't like stopping at pedestrian crossings and tend to speed up when they approach one, even if you have started to cross; they are extremely courteous when you are waiting to cross a street without a pedestrian crossing and will usually stop and wave at you to cross over!

Helpful Websites

I have already mentioned the help that we received from fellow members on the owners' forum. Here are a few websites that we found particularly useful.

www.nativespain.com – A good starting point, especially if you want to consider different regions in Spain. There are lots of interesting articles and blogs by people who are already living in Spain, which will give you a real insight into this fascinating country. Particularly useful if you want to get away from the costas and ex-pat way of life and enjoy the real Spain. Also look at their excellent range of books about life in Spain.

www.spain.info – This is the official website for tourism in Spain, which is a good tool when planning a holiday, but even more useful when you are researching different areas of Spain for potential places to live in.

www.eyeonspain.com – Another website that includes interesting articles, but is particularly good for the many forums dedicated to new developments. If you are considering buying off-plan check to see if other buyers from the development are on here, and find out if there are potential problems.

www.yeclaserve.com – This is a local website covering Yecla, Jumilla and the surrounding area. We have found its members very helpful in passing on local knowledge. However quirky your question, someone is bound to be able to answer it. Through this website we met Maria (the webmaster's wife) who speaks fluent English and has many years' experience helping ex-pats solve problems buying property in Spain. You can contact her at: maria@yeclaserve.com.

www.absolutespainforum.com – An interesting website as it covers many different areas in Spain and covers many topics.

www.costacalida.angloinfo.com - This is the section of the global AngloInfo website that covers the Costa Calida area, with helpful information for ex-pats living in Murcia. It also features blogs written by local ex-pats including "Jumilla Journal", Lisa's and my accounts of our life in Jumilla.

www.spainuncovered.com Whilst I am blowing my own trumpet, this is my personal blog, where I have continued writing about the ups and downs of our new life in Spain. The blog also gives tips about living and travelling in Spain for those of us on a budget.

www.kyero.com – This website gives you details about available property in Spain, plus the latest Spanish property news.

www.spanishpropertyinsight.com – This, not surprisingly, is another website dedicated to property in Spain. Well worth looking at before buying a property.

www.habitacasa.es – We rented the flat where we first stayed in Jumilla through habitacasa, and our agent Manuel also helped us find the flat we eventually bought there. The company deals with property on the coast around Santa Pola and La Manga, as well as property in Jumilla.

www.donpiso.com – A large chain of estate agents, with a local office in Jumilla, where their staff are very helpful too.

We decided to buy a furniture pack from Murcia Furniture as the quality of their furniture was good, and they allowed us to mix and match between the different packs to get exactly what we wanted. We could also have gone to the large Ikea in Murcia, but I must confess that I preferred not having to struggle with assembling our new furniture. It was much easier just walking into our new flat to discover that all the lights had been fitted, the curtains were hanging up, the glasses and crockery had been put away in the kitchen cupboards, and all the furniture was assembled with not a single flat-pack in sight! Of course it is cheaper to shop around and buy items from several different shops, which we did for electrical goods, and there are other furniture companies which may suit you better. If possible, try and get a personal recommendation.

Inmopinos' Estate Agent, Paseo De La Constitucion 36, Pinoso 03650, Alicante. Tel No: 0034 966970331, Fax No:

0034 966970372. This is the estate agent that John and Annette found very helpful.

I have kept one of the best to last, as whenever I need to know something about moving to or living in Spain and am uncertain where to find the information, I turn to good old Google: _www.google.co.uk_

One final word of warning though about using the internet: research widely on any topic that you need more information about and don't assume that the first website you look at is 100% accurate.

You also need to check how up-to-date that particular website is and remember that real life in Spain rarely bears any resemblance to life as described on the world wide web! We had coffee in a local café with Louise recently, and her view, based on her own experiences to date, is that everything in Spain is done back to front. No doubt you will have a lot of fun discovering whether this is true when you make your move to Spain.

Other Resources

Make friends with your local tourist office when visiting Spain and even after you have moved there. The staff in our tourist office know us well, and if we pop our head round the door they will tell us whether there are any new leaflets: that way we make sure that we don't miss any of the local fiestas and events.

There are many ex-pat newspapers, which also have websites, such as Costa Blanca News, Round Town News, Sur in English, Euro Weekly News, Spanish

Sun News, Essentials Marbella Magazine and The Inland Magazine.

These aren't the only ones, but they are the newspapers I have seen on a regular basis in different parts of Spain: just google them for more information.

I also recommend looking on Spanish websites such as *www.laverdad.es* to get the latest news in Spanish.

Public Transport

You will usually need to buy tickets at the ticket office, or from the ticket machine, before boarding a bus or train. It may very well cost you more if you wait to buy tickets on the train or from the bus driver.

Check your bus ticket carefully: if it has a time printed on it the ticket will only be valid on the bus that departs at that time. We have seen bus drivers refuse to accept a ticket with a different time on it. We have also seen drivers stop the bus and walk down the aisle to tell passengers to get off the bus when they have tried to go beyond the limit of their ticket.

If the ticket has a seat number you must sit in the allocated seat. Spanish passengers will stand patiently in the aisle until you vacate their seat. We have also noticed passengers walking down the bus looking for non-existent numbers on buses without seat numbers.

Expect the bus to be late, but don't rely on that as it may actually leave on time. You may even find that the timetable has changed without notice and it will go earlier than expected, so it pays to check with the bus station the day before.

If you see "locals" at a bus stop, don't assume that they know more than you do. You may find out too late that they are tourists too.

If you decide to splash out on first class travel on the train (preferente) and want a vegetarian or other special meal, you have to book it at least 24 hours in advance.

Many special offers on the train are only shown on the Spanish version of the RENFE website, so always check that as well as the English version.

If you are over 60 you can buy a Tarjeta Dorada for only 5.05 euros, which gives discounts of between 25% and 40% on local and national trains.

Some regions do special rates for pensioners on the buses, so remember to check it out. In Murcia, from time to time, they advertise free travel for everybody on the buses. Needless to say the bus station is always packed out when this happens!

Important Paperwork

In Spain, of course, all paperwork is important and I suggest that you invest in a large folder to keep the most vital documents in, as you will get nowhere without them. These are those you really can't live without:

- NIE number - Número de Identidad de Extranjero. This is a fiscal identity number, needed for buying or renting a property in Spain, as well as purchases such as a car.

Obtaining your NIE numbers should be one of the first things you do when you move to Spain, or even before you actually move there.

- Padrón. Once you are living in Spain, you then need to sign on the padrón, similar to the electoral roll in the UK. You will need your certificado de empadronamiento for many things, including registering at the centro de salud, and applying for your certificado de residencia.
- Certificado de residencia. If you are living in Spain permanently you are legally required to register at the National Police station for your area, which is not necessarily the nearest one. At the time of writing, in Murcia, you will need your NIE number, passport, certificado de empadronamiento and two passport photos. Remember the golden rule however: things do change in Spain from time to time, so check before you go!

Useful Telephone Numbers

It is worth finding out where your nearest local police station, Guardia Civil and health centre are, especially if you aren't living in the town centre. You don't want to have to wait for an emergency to realise that you don't know where they are, especially if your Spanish isn't that fluent.

Unique number for emergency services	112
Local ambulance service	061
Guardia Civil	062
Local police	092
National police	091

About Sue

Sue was born in Newcastle upon Tyne, in the Northeast of England, although she moved to Canada when she was eighteen months old. As a child she also lived in Norfolk and Lincolnshire, after her parents decided to return to England. At school her favourite subjects were English and French, however she also enjoyed sport even though she is not as talented a sportsperson as John is. She joined the WRNS when she left school as she wanted to travel, and she doesn't think "gap years" had been invented then! She played hockey and indoor football while serving in the WRNS, but didn't take up running until after marrying for the first time and having a family. She decided running was a cheap and easy sport for a busy mother of three children and much to her amazement actually enjoyed it. Sue had a variety of jobs after returning to work, mainly in IT and Personnel, as well as working for herself as a complementary therapist. Having thoroughly enjoyed writing this book, Sue is now keen to continue with her new career as a writer.

To connect with Sue and see loads of colour photos of her adventures in Spain visit her Facebook page: *www.facebook.com/profile.php?id=615274018*

About John

John was born in Portsoy in the Northeast of Scotland, although he moved to Armadale, halfway between Edinburgh and Glasgow, when he was eleven. He lived there until he joined the Army at seventeen and a half, serving in the Army around the world until the age of forty. He has always been a keen sportsman: he played cricket for his school, and also played football for Armadale Thistle and Hibernians Juniors while still at school. He took up running while he was in the Army, being a founder member of Serpentine Running Club, and he played a leading role in the running club after leaving the Army. John worked for the Metropolitan Police as a civilian until he retired and moved to Spain with Sue.

Seven Things You Never Knew About Sue & John

1. As well as not eating meat, Sue never eats tomatoes: her Mum said that even as a baby she didn't like them. John isn't fussy (he says), but refuses to eat coleslaw or celery.
2. Sue and John are non-drivers. Living in London there was no need to learn to drive, which is why they chose to live in a Spanish town with a good bus service.
3. Neither of them swims, which is a shame as there are several large outdoor pools plus one indoor pool in Jumilla. Are they too old to learn to swim now?

4. Sue and John have a collection of CDs from the 60s and 70s. When they got married recently, Sue chose "Don't stop me now" by Queen for the start of the ceremony, while John selected "Forever young" by Rod Stewart to be played when they left the room as a married couple.

5. John and Sue both learnt French at school, which of course is why they decided to live in Spain where most people speak Spanish.

6. John is a good cook and does most of the cooking at home. Sue likes to try out new recipes on the rare occasions when she enters the kitchen: her tortilla proved very successful, so she may venture there again!

7. Both Sue and John have an aversion to beach holidays, not just because they can't swim, but they like to be active and see the sights when they visit somewhere new. Their view is that beaches are meant for walking along, not for lazing in the sun.

Appendix

Useful Books

"Ghosts of Spain", Giles Tremlett, Faber. ISBN: 978-0-571-22168-4. This book goes a long way to helping you understand the Spanish people by looking at their history and culture.

"Living in Spain", Bill Blevins & David Franks, _www.blevinfranks.com_. Although this book isn't an easy read, we found it worthwhile for the essential financial, legal and other information it contained. Make sure that you get the latest edition though, as we know from our own experiences that things do change.

"A Place in the Sun Spain: A Guide to Buying and Living in Spain", Channel 4 Books, _www.booksattransworld.co.uk_. ISBN 1-905-02606-4. Ideal for a quick overview of Spain, with many hints for people thinking of moving to Spain, and covering several different areas.

"Eyewitness Travel: Spain", _www.dk.com_. 978-1-4053-1920-1. A good travel book that is revised annually, which is useful for finding out about the different regions within Spain both for holidays and potential places to live.

"Going Native in Murcia" (3rd edition), Marcus and Debbie Jenkins, NativeSpain.com, ISBN 978-1908770004. Written by people who really know the region as they actually live there, like other writers in the Native Spain series. Highly recommended, as we found lots of useful and fascinating information about the region we were moving to.

"Buying Property in Murcia", Debbie Jenkins, NativeSpain.com, ISBN 1-905430-29-9. Essential reading for anyone contemplating buying property in Murcia, but also very helpful for people buying elsewhere with its many tips on the buying process. I loved the Location-O-Meter, which enables you to quickly identify the location that meets your particular needs, and only wish the book had been published before we decided to buy a property in Spain.

"Going Native in Alicante", Susan Bearder, NativeSpain.com, ISBN 1-905430-36-1. Another gem in the Native Spain series, giving an insider's guide to Alicante that covered many of our favourite places, but also gave us new places to explore.

"Larousse diccionario compact english-spanish", _www.larousse.es_, ISBN 84-8332-672-8. We bought this in Murcia, so it is aimed at Spanish people learning English, however all sections are in English too. As we live inland, where very few people speak English, it has been an invaluable tool and is already well-thumbed.

"Collins Easy Learning Spanish Grammar", _www.collins.co.uk_, ISBN 0-00-719645-8. As our Spanish teacher doesn't speak English, this has also been invaluable as a back-up tool in helping us understand Spanish Grammar.

"Spain ... A Culinary Road Trip", Mario Batali with Gwyneth Paltrow, ecco, ISBN 978-0-06-156093-4. The companion book for the TV series "Spain … On The Road Again", with lots of interesting recipes from the regions they visited in the series.

"Modern Spanish Cooking", Sam and Eddie Hart, Quadrille, ISBN 978-1-84400-454-6. Described as "The best Spanish cookbook of recent times" and I'm not going to disagree, having successfully made tortilla with its help! Written by the owners of Fino, the outstanding Spanish restaurant, this book deserves to be in every ex-pat's kitchen as it will help you make the most of your delicious local produce.

Update on San José: April 2012

Nearly four years have passed since Herrada del Tollo (HdT), the company within the San José Group that was building Residencial Santa Ana del Monte, went into voluntary liquidation and we are no nearer to getting our deposit back.

The administrators produced their report at the end of 2008. Their recommendations for a scaled-down project of 1263 properties and a nine-hole golf course in phase one, with the hope that there would be later phases if the economic climate improved, were accepted by both the court and the creditors.

However things went from bad to worse when a shepherd took HdT to court, claiming that there was insufficient water to sustain the development, which would also put his own livelihood into jeopardy. The case eventually reached the Supreme Court in Madrid, who put a hold on the development going ahead until they had received the paperwork proving adequacy of resources. Unfortunately this paperwork did not reach the Supreme Court by the given date, so HdT now has to wait for the Court to sit and review the case.

Without a bank guarantee our expectations of recouping our losses are low, although under the agreement we are due 65% of our deposit back by 2015. This of course is dependent on the Supreme Court giving HdT the go ahead and the company subsequently obtaining the necessary finance.

A purchasers association was set up in 2008. Santa Ana del Monte Residents Cooperative (SARC) arranges regular meetings with HdT in order to keep purchasers informed of the latest developments: updates are posted on its website: www.santaanadelmonte.org/.

We know that we have been luckier than many of our fellow purchasers, as we have managed to buy another property in Jumilla where we are now living. If we do eventually get some of our deposit back we will look on that as a bonus. Some of our fellow purchasers have not been as fortunate and we can only hope that by telling our story we may prevent other couples from experiencing similar heartache.

Update on Sue and John: April 2012

If you have read this far, you will realise that things have moved on since I wrote the Prologue to this book at the beginning of 2009.

We have been living in our new flat on the outskirts of Jumilla since April 2009. Living with us is our dog Lisa, who kindly "adopted" us on 1 March 2010, which coincidentally was John's birthday.

We still go to our Spanish classes twice a week, though we are happy to report that our Spanish neighbours tell us our language skills are improving. Neither of us is convinced that we will ever master Spanish verbs though, especially as British friends who have lived here a lot longer than us find them just as difficult as we do.

Apart from learning Spanish we keep ourselves busy walking Lisa, writing two blogs (with a bit of help from Lisa), publicising events in Jumilla both in the ex-pat press and on the internet, organising a monthly English language book swap and a weekly intercambio (language exchange) with our British and Spanish friends. We also offer guided walks around Jumilla and visits to local bodegas through our "Walkers Tours of Jumilla". Whoever said it was easy being retired obviously hasn't retired yet!

Walkers Tours of Jumilla

Having retired to Jumilla we decided that we needed something to occupy ourselves, so we came up with the idea of providing free guided tours in English (or Scottish in John's case!)

We are happy to tailor the tour to suit your needs. If you love looking around museums, we can time it to allow you to have a leisurely browse around the Archeological Museum, the Ethnographic & Natural Science Museum and the Semana Santa (Holy Week) Museum.

If you prefer gardens and plazas to museums, a walk out to the Botanical Gardens can be included as well as a stroll to see the many lovely gardens and squares around the town. Jumilla castle is well worth visiting - if only for the amazing views. Although it is usually only open at weekends, we can arrange a guided tour during the week for a group of over twelve people.

A popular option at the end of the walk is a visit to one of Jumilla's many bodegas: after the tour of the bodega you can indulge yourself with wine-tasting and nibbles.

Please contact us through the website below if you want to book a tour or for further information about Jumilla.

www.spainuncovered.com/walkers-tours-guided-walks-around-jumilla/

Printed in Great Britain
by Amazon